Not for consumers

"Vitsœ's furniture does not shout; it performs its function in relative anonymity alongside furniture from any designer and in homes from any era. We make the effort to produce products like this for intelligent and responsible users – not consumers – who consciously select products that they can really use. Good design must be able to coexist."

Dieter Rams, 1976

VITSŒ

GRANTA

12 Addison Avenue, London W11 4QR | email: editorial@granta.com
To subscribe go to granta.com, or call 020 8955 7011 (free phone 0500 004 033)
in the United Kingdom, 845-267-3031 (toll-free 866-438-6150) in the United States

ISSUE 148: SUMMER 2019

PUBLISHER AND EDITOR	Sigrid Rausing
DEPUTY EDITOR	Rosalind Porter
POETRY EDITOR	Rachael Allen
DIGITAL DIRECTOR	Luke Neima
ASSISTANT EDITOR	Francisco Vilhena
SENIOR DESIGNER	Daniela Silva
DEPUTY ONLINE EDITOR	Eleanor Chandler
EDITORIAL ASSISTANT	Lucy Diver
OPERATIONS AND SUBSCRIPTIONS	Mercedes Forest
MARKETING	Aubrie Artiano, Simon Heafield
PUBLICITY	Pru Rowlandson
CONTRACTS	Isabella Depiazzi
TO ADVERTISE CONTACT	Charlotte Burgess, charlotteburgess@granta.com
FINANCE	Mercedes Forest, Josephine Perez
SALES MANAGER	Katie Hayward
IT MANAGER	Mark Williams
PRODUCTION ASSOCIATE	Sarah Wasley
PROOFS	Katherine Fry, Jessica Kelly, Lesley Levene, Louise Tucker
CONTRIBUTING EDITORS	Daniel Alarcón, Anne Carson, Mohsin Hamid, Isabel Hilton, Michael Hofmann, A.M. Homes, Janet Malcolm, Adam Nicolson, Edmund White

A comprehensive single-volume history of literature in the two major languages of Wales from post-Roman to post-devolution Britain.

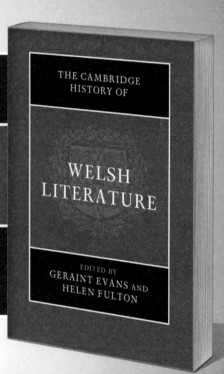

THE CAMBRIDGE HISTORY OF

WELSH LITERATURE

EDITED BY
GERAINT EVANS AND HELEN FULTON

'... *crammed with as many riches as a dragon's cave. Objective, superbly researched, it is the best book ever published about my homeland.*' Roger Lewis, *Daily Telegraph*

CONTENTS

THE SPREAD

Ben Lerner

Four hours later his alarm clock woke him. Half-asleep, he showered and put on the black suit he'd bought with his mom at West Ridge. He tied one of his father's two ties. He drove the short distance to Topeka High, pulling up beside his coaches, Spears and Mulroney, who were looking over an AAA map, their breath visible in the streetlight. The former was drinking coffee from his large thermos; the latter sipped, as ever, her Diet Coke. Other formally dressed adolescents wheeled large plastic tubs from the school and loaded them into the backs of two nearby vans. He did not condescend to move his own tub; an underclassman would take care of it. He saw his partner, Joanna, and nodded in greeting; they weren't friends; their alliance was purely tactical. Once in the van, she wanted to talk strategy, but he leaned his head against the cool window, watched the rise and fall of telephone wires in the dark, and soon he was moving through tract housing in his dreams. He woke up when they pulled off the highway to stop for breakfast at McDonald's, familiar contours of the molded seating.

Dawn was breaking as they arrived at Russell High School. He would normally have skipped such a small tournament, but because Russell was Bob Dole's hometown, and because Bob Dole was running for president, the Russell Invitational would this year draw the best teams from across the state; the logic was unclear to him, but Mulroney had insisted they attend. From similar district-issued vans and buses, other awkwardly costumed adolescents were unloading their own tubs, hauling them across the cold parking lot to the school's main entrance. When he and Joanna walked through the doors, their would-be competitors made way.

He found the high schools strangely altered on the weekends, the spaces transformed when emptied of students and teachers and severed from the rhythms of a normal day. The classrooms, with their hortatory posters, BE THE CHANGE YOU WANT TO SEE, their rows of empty desks, equations or dates or stock phrases left on chalk- or dry-erase boards, made Adam think of abandoned theatrical sets or photographs of Chernobyl. He could occasionally pick up traces of Speed Stick or scented lip gloss or other floating signatures of a social order now suspended. As they walked down the main hall of Russell High he tried various combinations on the lockers. He touched a wrestling state-championship banner hanging in the foyer with the distance of an anthropologist or ghost.

They gathered for a brief welcome assembly in a fluorescently lit cafeteria that smelled of industrial-strength bleach. The host coach made announcements while they looked over their brackets. Then the teams dispersed, carts of evidence in tow, to the assigned classrooms where a judge and timekeeper awaited.

He let Joanna lead him to their room. The daughter of two Foundation neurologists, Joanna was a short, smart, Ivy-bound senior who scored, as she would let you know, a 1600 on the SAT. She compiled almost all of their research, having attended a 'debate institute' at the University of Michigan over the summer to get a head start on the competition. (The topic this year was whether the federal government should establish new policies to reduce juvenile crime; their plan argued that strengthening child-support enforcement would do so in various ways.) Adam's contribution to prep work consisted of skimming *The Economist* during debate class. His strength was thinking on his feet, exposing fallacies; his cross-examinations were widely feared.

These early rounds were a formality; they dispatched low-ranked teams in front of lay judges, often the reluctant parents of other debaters. That weekend at Russell a couple of sophomores tried to surprise them by running a version of their own plan against them, having reconstructed it from notes taken during elimination rounds, which were open to spectators.

Adam rose, smoothing his father's tie, to cross-examine the obviously nervous first affirmative speaker; his opponent resembled a waiter in his white shirt, black slacks. They stood facing a judge – competitors do not look at one another – who could barely fit into the combination chair and desk; he sat with his arms crossed, glasses resting atop his bald head, begrudgingly making notes on a legal pad.

'Could you please repeat this year's resolution?'

'Repeat it?'

'Yes, please.'

'Resolved: that the government –'

'The *federal* government,' Adam says, as if he's embarrassed to have to help him. 'Take your time,' he adds, knowing it will sound like politeness to the judge, and to his opponent, infuriating condescension.

'Resolved: the federal government should establish a program to substantially reduce juvenile crime in the United States.' There's the slightest tremor in his voice.

'Why was child support established?'

'To support children, obviously' – the origin of the sarcasm is anxiety – 'after their parents get divorced.'

'Actually, unmarried parents accrue the same child-support obligations in most states.' Adam has no idea if what he's said is true. He makes a subtle show of ignoring, of transcending, his opponent's tone. 'But let's set that aside. It sounds like you agree the program you propose to strengthen was not primarily intended to substantially reduce juvenile crime.'

'No, I mean, that was among its intentions.'

'Do you have evidence supporting that assertion?' His tone makes it clear that he hopes his opponent does, that he would welcome that debate; it also communicates to the judge that the round is over if he doesn't. (The ballot instructs the judge that 'topicality' must be proved by the affirmative team. He and Joanna can crush these debaters in a variety of ways, but he'll start by seeing if his opponent trips himself up on this prima facie issue.)

'The evidence is that it cuts crime. That's why the advantages of our plan are –'

'So you're saying anything that has the effect of reducing crime is topical?'

'No. It has to be federal, a federal program.'

'So if I advocate that the federal government build nuclear power plants and it constructs them shoddily and that causes horrible pollution and the pollution produces disastrous health effects and mass death ensues and crime is thereby reduced, that's a topical resolution?' The judge smiles – both at what Adam's said and at his delivery. And he has reminded the judge of his distrust of the Feds.

'Of course not,' angry now.

'Why? Because it has to be an *intended* effect of the policy?'

'Okay, sure.'

'Do you have any evidence that this was an intended effect?'

'It's common sense.' He should argue that – regardless of *why* child support was established in general – they, the affirmative team, are now intending to expand the policy to reduce crime, arguably meeting the conditions of topicality. But he's too frazzled.

'I think what's common sense is that child support is designed to equalize financial burdens on parents following a separation. And that even if this equalization somehow *complicated* crime-reduction efforts, there would still be substantial arguments for its importance. And' – he realizes that, for the average citizen of Russell, Kansas, he might have just made a feminist argument; his pivot is without detectable hesitation – 'I can think of strong arguments against that kind of federal intervention in private relationships. The point is that's not the topic of this year's debate.'

'I – Look, you run this case all the time and topicality never –'

'Excuse me, I need to stop you there – you want the judge to award you this round because we have won other rounds with a similar case?' He's offended on behalf of debate itself.

'I'm not saying that. I'm –'

'That's an interesting idea, that what's argued in previous rounds should be relevant, can be used against us; should you lose this round arguing for the resolution since you presumably argued against it in a prior debate?' The judge is smiling again.

'No, of course not, but –'

'And, incapable of defending the topicality of your policy before the negative team' – he's deadly serious now, a prosecutor on *Law & Order* going in for the kill – 'you're bringing up the fact that you copied your plan from our affirmative rounds.' A pause. 'Your defense against failing to meet the burden of topicality is plagiarism?'

Brief silence in which the judge, eyebrows raised, makes a note.

'I'm just saying it's a topical plan,' he says meekly, the round already lost.

At Russell High it was not until the semifinals, when judging would be undertaken by a panel of three college debaters, that the competition really began. He and Joanna were on the affirmative side, facing a fairly formidable team from Shawnee Mission West. The room – a science classroom: microscopes on a big table in the corner, multiple sinks – was full: eliminated debaters and their coaches had become the audience. When the round was about to start, silence fell; for the first time Adam heard the aquarium filter running in a tank he hadn't noticed against the wall. He could just make out some slowly drifting yellow forms.

And now Joanna stands to deliver the first affirmative speech. For a few seconds it sounds more or less like oratory, but soon she accelerates to nearly unintelligible speed, pitch and volume rising; she gasps like a swimmer surfacing, or maybe drowning; she is attempting to 'spread' their opponents, as her opponents will attempt to spread them in turn – that is, to make more arguments, marshal more evidence than the other team can respond to within the allotted time, the rule among serious debaters being that a 'dropped argument', no matter its quality, its content, is conceded. (Competitive debaters spend hours doing speed drills – holding a pen in the teeth while reading, which forces the tongue to work harder, the mouth to over-enunciate; they practice reading evidence backward so as to uncouple the physical act of vocalization from the effort to comprehend, which slows one down.) The judges hunch over their legal pads, producing a flowsheet of the round along with the competitors, recording argument and counterargument in shorthand, making little or no eye contact with the speakers. During the brief intervals wherein their pens are idle, they twirl them around their thumbs, a signature habit of debaters.

To an anthropologist or ghost wandering the halls of Russell High School, interscholastic debate would appear less competitive speech than glossolalic ritual. See the cystic-acned first negative speaker from Shawnee Mission – his dress more casual, typical of the rich kids from Kansas City – reading evidence at 340 words per minute to support his claim that the affirmative plan will overburden family courts, setting off a catastrophic chain of events. He lets each page fall to the floor when he's finished, along with drops of sweat. He inhales sharply, shouts out another tag line – 'Overburdened courts lead to civil collapse' – then reads more evidence, getting briefly entangled in a stutter that, at such volume and such speed, makes it sound as though he's having a seizure or a stroke. As time runs out, he sums up his arguments, although few of the uninitiated could understand him: *Gregor evidence points to back-backlogged courts as result of increased child support enforcement judicial overload leads to civil collapse collapse leads to nuclear conflict China or North Korea nuclear strike in ensuing power vacuum out-out-outweighs whatever benefits affirmative plan offers and and and and Stevenson proves affirmative plan no solvency regardless because resistance from from internal agencies blocks imple-implementation must vote no on disadvantage impact alone but but even if you you consider plan as plan no solvency 1AC key source for Georgia courts not not applicable to fed program only state level so there is no way to vote but negative.*

The spread was controversial; if it happened in front of lay judges, there was shock, complaints. More than one highly ranked team had misjudged its judges and been eliminated in early rounds for speaking drivel. Old-timer coaches longed for the days when debate was debate. The most common criticism of the spread was that it detached policy debate from the real world, that nobody used language the way that these debaters did, save perhaps for auctioneers. But even the adolescents knew this wasn't true, that corporate persons deployed a version of the spread all the time: for they heard the spoken warnings at the end of the increasingly common television commercials for prescription drugs, when risk information was disclosed at a speed designed to make it difficult to comprehend; they heard the list of rules and caveats read rapid-fire at the end of promotions on the radio; they were at least vaguely familiar with the 'fine print' one received from financial institutions and health-insurance companies; the last thing one was supposed to do with those thousands of words was comprehend them. These types of disclosure were designed to conceal; they exposed you to information that, should you challenge the institution in question, would be treated like a 'dropped argument' in a fast round of debate – you have already conceded the validity of the point by failing to address it when it was presented. It's no excuse that you didn't have the time. Even before the twenty-four-hour news cycle, Twitter storms, algorithmic trading, spreadsheets, the DDoS attack, Americans were getting 'spread' in their daily lives; meanwhile, their politicians went on speaking slowly, slowly about values utterly disconnected from their policies.

Joanna was too fast for the Shawnee Mission kids; Adam spent most of the semifinal round pointing out which of her arguments his opponents had dropped. In the finals, when they were back on the negative side, they hit rivals from Lawrence High. When they'd lost to Rohan and Vinay in the past, it had been Adam's fault; they were as well prepared as Joanna. But that day, for whatever reason, his mind was particularly swift.

BEN LERNER

And that day at Russell High as he enumerated in accelerating
succession the various unpredictable ways implementation of his
opponents' plan would lead to nuclear holocaust (almost every plan,
no matter how minor, would lead to nuclear holocaust), he passed, as
he often passed, a mysterious threshold. He began to feel less like he
was delivering a speech and more like a speech was delivering him,
that the rhythm and intonation of his presentation were beginning to
dictate its content, that he no longer had to organize his arguments so
much as let them flow through him. Suddenly the physical tension he
carried was all focused energy, a transformation that made the event
slightly erotic. If the language coursing through him was about the
supposedly catastrophic effects of ending the government's Stingray
surveillance program or the affirmative speaker's failure to prove
solvency, he was nevertheless more in the realm of poetry than of
prose, his speech stretched by speed and intensity until he felt its
referential meaning dissolve into pure form. In a public school closed
to the public, in a suit that felt like a costume, while pretending to
argue about policy, he was seized, however briefly, by an experience
of prosody.

Then he was back in the cafeteria for the award ceremony, eating
Peanut M&M's a freshman had fetched him from the machine, half-
listening as Coach Spears tried to convince him that professional
wrestling was real: I've seen the blood; I've been close to the cage.
Adam nodded as he chewed. Everyone fell quiet when the host
coaches arrived to announce the final results and hand out medals.

But there was a commotion around the cafeteria doors. They
swung open and several reporters hurried in; a cameraman quickly
set up a bright light on a tripod, shouldered his camera. Then, to
the growing surprise of the assembled debaters, men who were
unmistakably bodyguards entered the room, looked around, coiled
tubes dangling from earpieces. He glanced at Coach Mulroney, who
displayed a knowing smile. Finally, Senator Bob Dole appeared, the
seventy-three-year-old Russell native who was less than a month
away from being crushed by Bill Clinton, a landslide victory for the

Democrat that would confirm that cultural conservatism was giving – had all but given – way to the reign of more liberal baby boomers. It would confirm that history had ended.

A few gasps of recognition, some applause. Dole, as ever, held a pen in his largely paralyzed right arm and waved his awkward wave with the left. He walked, flanked by aides, to the front of the cafeteria and shook the left hand of the host coach, who said, beaming, that the next president of the United States would be handing out the medals to the winners of this year's Russell High School Invitational. Before the medalists were recognized, Senator Dole wanted to say a few words.

'I'm not much of a debater myself,' he said, maybe expecting laughter, which didn't come, 'but I place great value on the skills that you are all developing here today.' Even for a politician, Dole spoke haltingly. (From his chair in the audience, Adam involuntarily pictured Dole holding the pen between his teeth, reading backward; he pictured Dole trying and failing to do the debater's twirl with the cold, incapable hand. Then he pictured his grandfather's paralyzed left arm in Rolling Hills.) 'You are the future leaders of America and I am very glad that you are all here improving your ability to communicate, to persuade. That's so important. In our democracy. Crucial. And learning so much about government and policy. Wonderful. I'm honored to get to be here and to let you know you're all winners in my book for the hard work you're doing. It will carry you far. Will be seeing some of you on Capitol Hill.'

He was given an index card from which he read the names of the third-place team, the debaters rising to accept their medals, pausing for photographs with the senator. He butchered Rohan's and Vinay's surnames; they stood almost apologetically.

Now I am going to show you a picture and I'd like you to make up a story about it. We call this the Thematic Apperception Test, or TAT. A story with a beginning, a middle and an end. It's a black-and-white photograph that appeared on the front page of the *Topeka Capital-Journal*. (Who is this unsmiling seventeen-year-old boy whose hair is drawn into a ponytail while the sides of his head are shaved, a disastrous tonsorial compromise between the lefty household of his parents and the red state in which he was raised? His left hand is almost touching Dole's right, which clutches the pen; around his neck the teenager wears a medal won by speaking a nearly private language at great speed. The senator, who often refers to himself in the third person, whose campaign is advised by Paul Manafort, will be the only former presidential candidate to attend the Republican convention in 2016.) What are these people in this picture thinking? Feeling? Start by telling me what led up to this scene. ■

Unplug

yourself

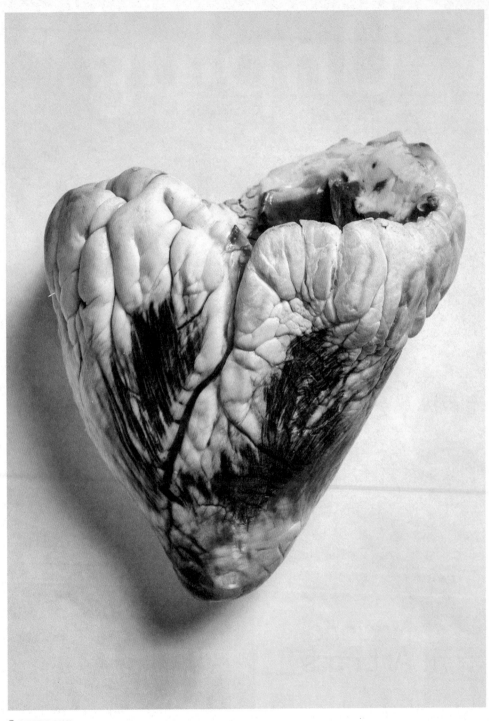

© JENNIFER MAY
Beef Heart, 2017

INNARDS

Magogodi oaMphela Makhene

Everyone claims ancestral royalty. Even slaves. No one imagines their beginning as damned or marred by mediocrity. No. The likely telling is of glory. Of kings and paramount chiefs prostrating themselves like bush rabbits in fear of our fathers, those fearsome foxes. Of queen mothers throwing their first-born daughters into our bloodstream like eager spawn sifting salt water for sperm.

— Our star was born long-tailed, the old man liked to say. We were kingmakers and twin sires. Even our cows came in pairs. We made rain fall in Great Zimbabwe.

No one asks him, How then, did the Boers and the British happen? How did such a strong and certain seed turn slave in its ancestral land?

So much of who we are is fiction. The old man's wife used to tell him that. That only Woman could be God. Only Woman – who takes heat, sweat and sin and turns it into flesh; into sacred being. Carrying life teaches you that, she'd say. Maybe that's why history forgets our grandmothers. They are written in the womb.

The morning the old man died, his firstborn heard him rise. Early. Said she could hear his mattress slump, fatigued. It was his heart that did him. Naledi woke before him, before the sun. Thought nothing of the laden quiet entering the house with first light as she filled the kettle, eager water hissing in a narrow stream.

The old man sat on his bed, hand to heart.

He knew so many things about the heart. He knew the shape and smell of the organ lying in a cardboard box at the slaughterhouse. The boxes went for nothing in the beginning, when he first started peddling unwanted dog meat earmarked for the dump. But then the abattoir figured if a muscled-up and capable darkie was willing to wait religiously for butcher-block dregs week after week, there was obviously some kaffir market out there worth cashing in on. Price tags latched onto the boxes. Soon, picking out the right bin without finding something spoiling at the bottom became Ntatemogolo's point of pride.

To pick the right heart, the old man said, you had to look for depth in the ruby, to prize a raw intensity of colour and a bright gold fat blanketing the angry muscle. He tried passing this along to his one son and double daughters. But they were repelled by his trade, wounded by its poverty. So he kept his motherwit to himself until the younger lot, the great-grandchildren especially, wanted to know what Ntatemogolo remembered. Was it true his grandfathers' grandfathers enkindled rainfall for the royal crops in Great Zimbabwe? That they burst clouds open merely by chanting their clan's praise names? Was it true Ntatemogolo could *still* coax a heart from its secret cavity and hold it in his hand so it throbbed like a newborn? Yes! Ntatemogolo would beam, Yes, it's true! You have to cradle it so its blood becomes your blood. So its arteries feel like they're pumping through *your* valves, like fresh blood is still brewing in its deepest heart of hearts.

It wasn't hard for his great-grandchildren to picture this. Until the day he died, their Ntatemogolo sold innards – beastly bits of waste food no one wanted. Pork fatback and leaf lard. Sheep guts and wormy kidney. Chicken feet. Beef tongue. Bird brain and beak and vulval-pink sweetbreads Ntatemogolo claimed could power unthinkable virility. He wedged his wares into a shabby bicycle basket that doubled as wandering butchery for the poorest among an already impoverished underclass – old women who picked out fleas and stray hairs from his newspapered packages; already tar-toothed man-children afraid of losing another limb to the mines. Flies loved the old man, sampled everything in his path and buzzed excitedly about his balding hairline, his pungent overalls and weathered veldskoens.

He wore a daily uniform that hadn't changed in over forty years: blue overalls, white undershirt and a brown wool balaclava for the meanest days. He bought a new pair of overalls for each weekday after his son started working, and only because that son, Modise, burned his first pair. Modise would've burned the old man's bicycle too, had it not been for Naledi.

She'd hobbled towards Modise and body-slammed the full force of her limp dead weight against his narrow frame. Into the bicycle they crashed, Modise more bewildered than beaten. Still, he paid with sixteen stitches across his temple and a whole week's pay for five new overalls. No one made him buy all five, but the sting of a woman beating him in broad daylight, and a crippled one at that – and maybe even the raging shame that chafed him into ransacking their father's business in the first place – it all drove Modise to replace the one worn overalls with five. The bicycle he left alone. Besides, it still worked, and the old man was attached to it, even if it wobbled and threatened to flatten everything in sight.

It was born rusty, Ntatemogolo's bike. Part of Modise's shame. Bombed-out metallic debris on wood wagon wheels with a ramshackle kind of rust. Made in England. Probably in Coventry, back when Europe was a Chinese factory floor and the colonies supplied a hungry market for every imperial reject the mother country spawned. No one could have predicted the old man's fate back then: death after a desperate century eking out an unyielding life, canned grief following four stillborns and the internal inferno of having failed the three who somehow survived. And then the end – a dry-throated longing for a dead wife, not the two passionate love affairs he'd piously nursed and coddled in the thick of his marriage.

He was a child when the bike was assembled. A herdboy who learned his numbers counting cows. Five hundred and ninety-five cattle.

Sheep, goats and fowl besides. His job was tallying every cow with every sunset and knowing which was who by name. It was the beginning of the Great Wars. Ntatemogolo was barefoot and still teething; General Jan Smuts a conniving double-dealer rallying his reluctant Boer brethren to fight for king and country. The same king and country Smuts had taken on in not one, but two bloody Anglo-Boer wars. You can forget it, the hardliners told him. But Smuts was a clever Boer. He flushed out his fellow Afrikaners' pro-German anti-Brit rebellion and sold it back to them as good politics – after all, what's a little filth to fine fellows? Of course, in Ntatemogolo's family compound and cosmos, all that seemed far away. As if the Boers and coming wars would never touch them. As if another country, another manhood lay very close ahead – someplace inevitable for this black herdboy. Rainmaking and black kings reigning – all that still seemed wildly possible.

But by the end of both Great Wars, Elias, as Ntatemogolo was known back then, had lost everything. His father, a menial soldier digging trenches for king and country – a glorified war mule in the South African Native Labour Corps – did not return from France. The family farm, a plump parcel on rich red earth, never stood a chance against the kleptocratic claws of Afrikaner power that soon clutched the country. The father who never returned, who fought for the British believing their promises of Native advancement *after* the war, his absence was all the state needed to declare his land unoccupied – fallow and fertile land fit for white occupation. They gave his wife twenty-one days to cease and desist. Of course she could keep her cows, they scoffed. Five hundred and ninety-five cattle. Three hundred sheep. Forty-two lambs and ninety-eight goats. What woman could possibly manage all that? But either for native stubbornness or new-found grief, she marched those beasts across stolen farms. Somehow, Elias's mother corralled the herd to a faraway uncle who promised protection and freedom. But very soon, as soon as the last hoof crossed into his kraal, that uncle counted every horned head and twin calves – every single beast – a new debt the young widow owed.

One hundred years later, the herdboy's heart stops. He feels its murmur slurring as he sits up, hand to chest, Naledi humming in the kitchen.

If anyone knew what signs to look for, if the line and land between his forebears and children remained unbroken, unstolen, someone would've heard the stars piercing sky the night before. They would've begun preparations for the old man's passing the way his own mother had known to tend to her affairs a distant century earlier, long before word reached that her husband would never return. They would've understood that long-tailed stars don't weep across the sky for celestial vanity. That the stars were mourning their blood.

But Ntatemogolo's children are scattered across oceans. They've long lost their ties to the shallow grave dug after Ntatemogolo's birth. To the clumps of soil, gravel and clay entombing his umbilical cord. To the earth tethering his creation to his mother's, whose birth rope is also buried in that pit, connecting every strain of blood coursing between generations . . . all the way back to that first ancestral womb.

But none of them can read the signs. Few understand how a shabby man in shabby overalls bicycling his stinky business around dusty streets could possibly be chosen. *Chosen?* Naledi would have snorted. *Chosen for what?*, her mind already unravelling the dirt-poor youth it had squirrelled away. None of Ntatemogolo's children could smell the iron stars smelted into their blood. And so, when Naledi limps into the room, her dead foot brushing broom-like across the floor, all she sees is her father seated on the bed.

Strange, she thinks. He's normally dressed and worrying his wispy whiskers with that blunt razor by now. His everyday porridge thickens on the stove. She smells its sour tartness, the strong fermented scent of tieng curdling the room. The curtains are drawn. Morning light still tepid.

— *Le tsogile*, Ntate? Naledi asks her father.

The old man does not respond, *Yes, we have risen.* Instead, he tries to heave his weight upright. Bony elbows, bare naked and tightening chest.

Naledi rounds the bed and approaches the window. Opens the brass metal latch, breathes in brisk morning air. Still sitting, Elias – or George as he later preferred people say – feels Naledi move behind him, sees her crooked spine. Can see it in the mirror and imagine it without looking. She would've been a carbon copy of her mother, he often thinks to himself. If not for the fall. She would have become the unfettered thing he once felt pulsing in his hands when he first saw his wife: *naledi* – true star. The grip in his chest tightens. Ntatemogolo releases his hand and slumps back on the bed. He doesn't mean to frighten her, but the sudden thud startles Naledi. She turns around expectedly. She thinks she'll find something hard and heavy free-falling. A misplaced phone directory, maybe, or those old boots Ntatemogolo likes to store above the wardrobe. She hears hard gasps for breath instead, lungs fighting to expand, as if her father's exhalations can support more life in the open air. She kneels at the foot of the bed and leans in. *Ntate?* She repeats, *Father?* She shakes his arm, frightened by its lightness. Her father isn't fighting but his face registers tension and his hand creeps back over his heart.

—What is it? Naledi asks. *Ntate!* Please, *bathong* – let me get an ambulance.

She steadies her good arm to lift herself off the floor. Ntatemogolo grabs her hand. *Stay,* his grip says. Naledi leans deeper into her functional hand, edging closer on the bed, sitting nearer, right beside him, right on the spot where her mother's head used to rest. She tries to hear what his eyes speak. He's calm. Zero panic. No last-minute flutter for flight or furious rush of words.

I'm leaving. He thinks maybe he should say, but decides it is self-apparent. So he speaks instead to his heart, fights for calm through its sudden rage. It's okay, he wants to say. Naledi weeps. *Smile,* he instructs himself, but a sharp pain shoots through his left arm and he feels his heart rupture like lightning splitting its prey. He closes his eyes.

Naledi's tears, her face now hovering over his, splatter stupidly onto his skin. His hand still holds hers and even though she senses danger, his grip fastens, clamping down as if the old dying man could crush her to the bone. *It's just a scare*, she thinks, reaffirming this to herself as his eyes reopen, as Ntatemogolo manages a smile. *And he is still breathing!* A soft sound stammering from the old man; a sigh.

—*You're going to live*, she thinks, speaking it out loud. He smiles again, a narrow smile, his lips taut as his eyes flicker gently, a century's weight beating heavy against his lids. His heart, tired now but still roaring, claps a faint echo he alone can hear.

Everything fades. Dizziness floods his vision with the sudden intensity of morning light. Millions of microscopic cells that have mended his heart through love and loss, through stolen joys and naked humiliation, are now starving for oxygen. His hand slackens. The muscle's electricity flashes a final warning. Ntatemogolo opens his eyes one last time, his heart at final drumbeat. It is not Naledi's broken body and shattered face he sees, it is her mother's. His wife. Not a ghost. George does not believe in ghosts. It is her spirit. A full, self-sustaining light. The electricity in his heart reroutes, grounds into earth. Naledi closes her father's eyes and lets out a sharp wail. ∎

THE LINE

Amor Towles

1

During the last days of the last tsar, there lived a peasant named Pushkin in a small village one hundred miles from Moscow. Though Pushkin and his wife, Irina, had not been blessed with children, they had been blessed with a cozy two-room cottage and a few acres that they farmed with the patience and persistence appropriate to their lot. Row by row they would till their soil, sow their seeds and harvest their crops – moving back and forth across the land like a shuttle through a loom. And when their workday was done, they would journey home where they would dine on cabbage soup at a little wooden table and then succumb to the holy sleep of the countryside.

Though the peasant Pushkin did not share his namesake's facility with words, he was something of a poet in his soul – and when he witnessed the leaves sprouting on the birch trees, or the thunderstorms of summer, or the golden hues of autumn, he would feel in his heart that theirs was a satisfactory life. In fact, so satisfactory was their life, had Pushkin uncovered an old bronze lantern while tilling the fields and unleashed from it an ancient genie with three wishes to grant, he wouldn't have known what to wish for.

And we all know exactly where that sort of happiness leads.

2

Like many of Russia's peasants, Pushkin and his wife belonged to a *mir* – a cooperative that leased the land, allocated the acres and shared expenses at the mill. On occasion, the members of the *mir* would gather to discuss some matter of mutual concern. At one such meeting in the spring of 1916, a young man who had traveled all the way from Moscow took to the podium in order to explain the injustice of a country in which 10 percent of the people owned 90 percent of the land. In some detail, he described the means by which capital had sweetened its own tea and feathered its own nest. In conclusion, he encouraged all assembled to wake from their slumbers and join him in the march toward the inevitable victory of the international proletariat over the forces of repression.

Pushkin was not a political man, or even a particularly educated man. So, he did not grasp the significance of everything this Muscovite had to say. But the visitor spoke with such enthusiasm and made use of so many colorful expressions that Pushkin took pleasure in watching the young man's words go by just as one would the flags on an Easter Sunday flotilla.

That night, as Pushkin and his wife walked home, they were both quiet. This struck Pushkin as perfectly appropriate given the hour and the delicate breeze and the chorus of crickets singing in the grass. But if Irina was quiet, she was quiet the way a heated skillet is quiet – in the moments before you drop in the fat. For while Pushkin had enjoyed watching the young man's words drift by, Irina's consciousness had closed upon them like the jaws of a trap. With an audible snap, she had taken hold and had no intention of letting go. In fact, so tight was her grip on the young man's arguments that, should he ever want them back, he would have to gnaw through his own phrases the way a wolf in a trap gnaws through its ankle.

3

The wisdom of the peasant is founded on one essential axiom: while wars may come and go, statesmen rise and fall, and popular attitudes wax and wane, when all is said and done a furrow remains a furrow. Thus, Pushkin witnessed the war years, the collapse of the monarchy and the rise of Bolshevism with the judicious perspective of Methuselah. And once the hammer and sickle were flapping over Mother Russia, he was ready to pick up his plow and resume the work of life. So, he was utterly unprepared for the news his wife delivered in May of 1918 – that they were moving to Moscow.

'Moving to Moscow,' said Pushkin. 'But why on earth would we be moving to Moscow?'

'Why?' demanded Irina with a stamp of the foot. 'Why? Because the time has come!'

In the pages of nineteenth-century novels, it was not uncommon for the lovely young ladies raised in the countryside to long for a life in the capital. After all, that is where the latest fashions could be seen, the latest dance steps learned and the latest romantic intrigues discussed sotto voce. In a similar manner, Irina longed to live in Moscow because that's where the factory workers swung their hammers in unison and the songs of the proletariat could be heard from every kitchen door.

'No one pushes a monarch over a cliff to celebrate the way things were,' proclaimed Irina. 'Once and for all, the time has come for Russians to lay the foundations of the future – shoulder to shoulder and stone by stone!'

When Irina articulated her position to her husband, using all of these words and many more, did Pushkin argue? Did he give voice to the first thoughts of hesitation that leapt into his head? He did not. Instead, he began carefully, thoughtfully formulating a rebuttal.

Interestingly, as Pushkin's position began to take shape, it drew upon the very same words that Irina's had: *The time has come.* For he was no stranger to this phrase. In fact, he was practically its closest relative. Since Pushkin was a boy, the phrase had roused him in the morning and tucked him in at night. 'The time has come to sow,' it would say in spring, as it opened the shutters to let in the light. 'The time has come to reap,' it would say in fall, as it lit the fire in the stove. The time has come to milk the cows, or bale the hay. That is, the time has come – not once and for all, but once again – to do that which one has always done in the manner of the sun, the moon and the stars.

This was the rebuttal that Pushkin began formulating that first night when he doused the lantern and climbed into bed. He continued formulating it the next morning when he walked with his wife through the dewy grass on their way to the fields. And he was formulating it still in the fall of that year when they loaded their wagon with all their possessions and set out for Moscow.

4

On 8 October, the couple arrived in the capital after five days on the road. As they rattled their way along the thoroughfares, we need not belabor their every impression: their first sight of a streetcar, of streetlamps, of a six-story building; of bustling crowds and expansive shops; of fabled landmarks like the Bolshoi and the Kremlin. We needn't belabor any of that. It is enough to state that their impressions of these sights were diametrically opposed. For while in Irina they stirred a sense of purpose, urgency and excitement, in Pushkin they stirred only dismay.

Having reached the city center, Irina didn't waste a minute to recover from their journey. Telling Pushkin to wait with the wagon, she quickly got her bearings and disappeared into the crowd. By the end of the first day, she had secured them a one-room apartment in the Arbat where, in place of a portrait of the tsar, she hung a photograph of Vladimir Ilich Lenin in a brand-new frame. By the end of the second day, she had unpacked their belongings and sold their horse and wagon. And by the end of the third, she had secured them both a job at the Red Star Biscuit Collective.

Formerly owned by Crawford & Sons of Edinburgh (Bakers to the Queen since 1856), the Red Star Biscuit Collective was housed in a 50,000-square-foot facility with 500 employees. Behind its gates it boasted two silos of grain and its own flour mill. It had mixing rooms with giant mixers, baking rooms with giant ovens, and packing rooms with conveyor belts that carried the boxes of biscuits right into the backs of the idling trucks.

Irina was initially assigned as an assistant to one of the bakers. But when an oven door came loose, she proved herself so adept with a monkey wrench that she was immediately transferred to the in-house engineers. Within a matter of days, it was commonly said that Irina could tighten the bolts of the conveyors as they rolled along without interruption.

Meanwhile, Pushkin was assigned to the mixing room where the biscuit batter was blended by paddles that clanged against the sides of large metal bowls. Pushkin's job was to add the vanilla to each batch of biscuits whenever a green light flashed. But having carefully dispensed the vanilla into the appropriate measuring cup, the noise of the machinery was so deafening and the motion of the paddles so hypnotic, Pushkin simply forgot to pour the flavoring in.

At four o'clock, when the official taster came to taste, he didn't even need to take a bite to know that something was amiss. He could tell from the aroma. 'What good is a vanilla biscuit that has no taste of vanilla?' he inquired of Pushkin, rhetorically, before sending an entire day's output to the dogs. And as for Pushkin, he was reassigned to the sweeping crew.

On his first day with the sweepers, Pushkin was sent with his broom to the cavernous warehouse where the sacks of flour were stacked in towering rows. In all his life, Pushkin had never *seen* so much flour. Of course, a peasant prays for an ample harvest with enough grain to last the winter, and maybe a bit left over to protect against a drought. But the sacks of flour in the warehouse were so large and piled so high, Pushkin felt like a character in a folk tale who finds himself in the kitchen of a giant where mortal men are dropped into a pie.

However daunting the environment, Pushkin's job was simple enough. He was to sweep up any flour that had spilled on the floor when the dollies were whisked to the mixing room.

Perhaps it was the general sense of agitation that Pushkin had been feeling since his arrival in the city; perhaps it was the memory of swinging a scythe, a motion that Pushkin had happily performed since his youth; or perhaps it was a congenital muscular disorder that had yet to be diagnosed. Who can say? But whenever Pushkin attempted to sweep the flour that had fallen to the floor, rather than push it into the pan, his motion would kick it into the air. Up it would go in a large white billow settling like a dusting of snow on his shoulders and hair.

'No, no!' his foreman would insist, as he grabbed the broom from Pushkin's hands. 'Like this!' And in a few quick strokes the foreman would clear four square feet of flooring without setting a single mote of flour into flight.

A man who was eager to please, Pushkin watched his foreman's technique with the attention of a surgical apprentice. But as soon as the foreman had turned his back and Pushkin had set his broom to the ground, up into the air the flour went. Such that after three days on sweeping detail, Pushkin was dismissed from the Red Star Biscuit Collective altogether.

'Dismissed!' shouted Irina that night in their little apartment. 'How does one get fired from Communism!'

In the days that followed, Irina might have tried to answer this question, but there were gears to be adjusted and screws to be tightened. What's more, she had already been elected to the workers' committee at the factory – where she was known to boost the morale of her comrades by quoting from *The Communist Manifesto* at the drop of a hat. In other words, she was a Bolshevik through and through.

And Pushkin? He rolled about the city like a marble on a chessboard.

5

With the ratification of the new constitution in 1918, it was the dawn of the Proletarian Age. It was also a period of the rounding up of enemies, the forced procurement of agricultural output, the prohibition of private trade and the rationing of essentials. Well, what did you expect? A frosted cake and your pillows fluffed by a housemaid?

Between her twelve-hour shift at the plant and her duties on the workers' committee, Irina hadn't a minute to spare. So, as she was headed off one morning, she thrust the ration cards for bread, milk and sugar into her idle husband's hands and told him, in no uncertain terms, to replenish the cupboards before she returned at ten o'clock that night. Then she pulled the door shut with such force that Vladimir Ilich swung on his hook.

As Irina's shoes sounded down the stairs, our hero stood where she had left him staring wide-eyed at the door. Without moving, he listened to her exit the building and walk to the trolley. He listened to the trolley clatter through the city and the sound of the whistle as Irina marched through the gates of the collective. Only when he heard the conveyor belts beginning to roll did it occur to Pushkin to utter the phrase 'Yes, dear'. Then, with the ration tickets firmly in hand, he donned his cap and ventured out into the streets.

As he walked along, Pushkin anticipated his task with a certain amount of dread. In his mind's eye, he could see a crowded shop where Muscovites pointed, shouted and shoved. He could see a wall of shelves lined with brightly colored boxes and a counterman who asked what you wanted, told you to be quick about it, then set the wrong thing down on the counter with a definitive thump before shouting, '*Next!*'

Imagine Pushkin's surprise when he arrived at the bakery on Battleship Potemkin Street – his first scheduled stop – and found the setting as quiet as a crèche. In place of the pointing, shouting and shoving there was a line, an orderly line. Composed mostly of women between the ages of thirty and eighty, it stretched gracefully from the doorway and made its way politely around the bend.

'Is this the line for the bakery?' he asked an older woman.

Before she could answer, another standing nearby gestured forcibly with her thumb. 'The end of the line is at the end of the line, comrade. In the back of the back.'

Offering his thanks, Pushkin turned the corner and followed the line three whole blocks to the back of the back. Having dutifully taken his place, Pushkin learned from the two women in front of him that the bakery offered each customer only one product: a loaf of black bread. While the women reported this news in annoyance, Pushkin was heartened by it. If there was only one loaf of black bread per customer, there wouldn't have to be any squinting or selecting or thumping down of items. Pushkin would wait in line, receive his loaf and bring it home, just like he'd been instructed.

As Pushkin was having this thought, a young woman appeared at his side.

'Is this the end of the line?' she asked.

'It is!' exclaimed Pushkin with a smile, glad to have the chance to be of service.

In the next two hours, Pushkin advanced as many blocks.

For some of us, maybe most of us, the ticking of these minutes would have sounded like the drip from a faucet in the middle of the night. But not for Pushkin. His time in the line made him no more anxious than would the wait for a seedling to sprout or the hay to change hue. Besides, while he waited he could engage the women around him in one of his favorite conversations.

'It is a beautiful day, isn't it?' he said to the four of them. 'The sun could not be shining more brightly, nor the sky a bluer shade of blue. Although, in the afternoon, I suspect we may be in for a bit of rain . . .'

The weather! I hear you exclaim with a roll of the eyes. *This is his favorite conversation?*

Yes, yes, I know. When God the Father is smiling on a nation, when average incomes are on the rise, food is plentiful and soldiers are biding their time with card games in their barracks, nothing seems worthier of condescension than a discussion of the weather. At dinner parties and afternoon teas, those who routinely turn to the topic are deemed boring, even insufferable. The possibility of precipitation seems worthy as a topic only to those without the imagination or intelligence to speak of the latest literature, the cinema and the international situation – or, in short, *the times*. But when a society is in turmoil, a discussion of the weather doesn't seem quite so insufferable . . .

'Why, yes,' agreed one of the women with a smile. 'It is a beautiful day.'

'Though,' observed another, 'it does seem from the clouds behind the cathedral that you might be right about the rain.'

And, just like that, the time seemed to pass a little more quickly.

At 1 p.m. that afternoon (with his loaf of bread tucked under his coat) Pushkin made his way to Maxim Gorky Street, where he had been instructed to obtain the sugar. Once again, he felt a flash of anxiety as he neared the shop, though this time the anxiety was countered by the slightest hint of hope. And what did he find when he arrived at his destination? By the grace of God, another line!

Naturally, as it was later in the day, the line at the grocer's was longer than the one at the bakery had been. But the brief rain which, in fact, had fallen on Moscow from 12.15 to 12.45, had cooled the streets and freshened the air. And as Pushkin approached, two women he had met in the bread line gave him a friendly wave. So, he took his place with a general sense of well-being.

Across the street from where Pushkin was standing happened to be the Tchaikovsky Conservatory, as fine an example of neoclassical architecture as existed in all of Russia.

'Isn't that building delightful,' Pushkin said to an old woman who had joined him at the end of the line. 'Just look at those scrolly things at the top of the columns, and the little statues tucked beneath the eaves.' And she, who had lived in the neighborhood for over forty years and who had passed the building a thousand times without giving it a second thought, had to admit, upon closer consideration, that it was nothing short of delightful.

Thus, time in the grocery line also began to pass a little more quickly. In fact, it passed so quickly that Pushkin hardly noticed the afternoon slipping away . . .

That night when Irina returned home, Pushkin was standing by the door in such a state of trepidation that the second she saw him she let out an anticipatory sigh.

'What has happened now?' she demanded.

Having the good sense not to mention the fine weather, or the architecture of the conservatory, or the friendly women whom he'd met, Pushkin explained to his wife that the lines for bread and sugar had been so long that there hadn't been time to wait in the line for milk.

When Pushkin held out the bread and sugar as evidence of his best intentions, he could see his wife clench her jaw, lower her eyebrows and close her fists. But even as Pushkin prepared for the worst, he saw his wife's eyeballs begin to shift. Suddenly, she found herself wrestling with her husband's failure to complete three simple tasks on the one hand and the implied shortcomings of Communism on the other. Were she to express her anger at Pushkin, wouldn't that in some way suggest her acknowledgment of the unacceptability of having to wait in line for one's bread and sugar and milk? Were she to cuff him on the head, wouldn't she to some degree be cuffing the revolution? Sometimes, one plus one does not so easily sum to two.

'Very good, husband,' she said at last. 'You can get the milk tomorrow.'

And in that moment, Pushkin felt a great sense of joy. For to serve the ones we love and receive their approval in return, need life be any more complicated than that?

6

It didn't take long for the citizens of Moscow to realize that if you had no choice but to stand in line, then Pushkin was the man to stand next to. Graced with a gentle disposition, he was never boorish or condescending, neither full of opinions nor full of himself. Once he had commented on the fineness of the weather or the beauty of a building, he was most likely to ask about your children. And so sincere was his interest that his eyes would brighten with satisfaction at the first suggestion of a success and cloud with tears at any hint of a setback.

While for his part, Pushkin had settled into city life with a growing sense of contentment. Waking in the mornings, he would take a glance at the calendar and think, *Ah, it is Tuesday. The time has come to wait in line for bread.* Or *Is it already the 28th? Once again, the time has come to go to Yakusky Street to wait in line for tea.* And thus, the months would have run into years and the years into decades without cause for remark, but for an unanticipated occurrence in the winter of 1921.

On the afternoon in question, after waiting three hours for a head of cabbage, Pushkin was about to proceed to a small department store on Tverskaya Street to wait for two spools of thread when an acquaintance hailed him from the back of the cabbage line. A thirty-year-old mother of four, she was clearly in a state of distress.

'Nadezhda!' our hero proclaimed. 'What is it?'

'It is my youngest,' she replied. 'He is bedridden with a fever. And while I need to pick up a head of cabbage for my family's soup, I fear that where I should be standing is in the line at the pharmacy!' Pushkin's expression reflected all the anxiety in this poor woman's heart. He looked to the sky and noted from the position of the sun – which was dipping behind the rooftops – that while Nadezhda would have time for one line or the other, she would never have time for both. Without a second thought, Pushkin looked to the eight women behind Nadezhda (who had all been leaning forward to hear the exchange).

'Perhaps these fine ladies wouldn't mind if I were to hold your place while you visited the pharmacy. As it is Tuesday, the line there shouldn't be too long. And once you've obtained Sasha's medicine, you could hurry back and resume your spot.'

Now, were you or I to have had made this simple suggestion, it would almost certainly have been met with looks of disdain and a reminder that a line is a line, not a carousel that you can hop on and off to your heart's content! But, at one time or another, all of these women had waited with Pushkin and experienced his gentleness of spirit. So, without objection, they made room for him as the young mother hurried away.

Just as Pushkin had anticipated, the line at the pharmacy was only thirty people long. So, when Nadezhda reached the cash register with the medication in hand, feeling a burst of goodwill she splurged on a bag of brightly colored candy sticks. And when she resumed her place in the cabbage line, she overcame Pushkin's objections and insisted that he take a handful of the confections as a token of her gratitude.

7

Times of upheaval throw off orphans like sparks. Wherever the grinder meets the metal, they shoot in the air in dazzling arcs, then either bounce once on the pavement and disappear or settle in the hay and smolder. On a morning in 1923, one such castoff – a boy named Petya – sat on the cold stone steps of a decommissioned church with his elbows on his knees and his chin in his palms as he aimlessly watched the breadline across the street.

To the uninitiated, a breadline might seem a promising spot for an urchin. After all, most of those waiting were women who had cared for offspring of their own – an experience that was almost certain to trigger feelings of compassion toward a motherless child. Well, maybe so. But as Petya could tell you from experience, young lads who approached the women in the breadline with their hands outstretched received a twist of the ear.

On this particular morning, while Petya eyed the progress of the women with the watchful resignation of a well-trained dog, something extraordinary caught his attention. As a man near the front of the line was chatting amiably with the women at his side, a young wife in a yellow kerchief appeared from around the corner with a bag in her arms. When she approached, the man doffed his cap, greeted her warmly and stepped out of the line in order to give her his place.

Now, if the mothers in the breadline were prone to twist the ear of an orphan, they were sure to give a line-cutter a dressing-down she'd not soon forget. But the women didn't shout or shake their fists. They made room for the newcomer. Then, as the man in the cap bid them all goodbye, the young wife reached into her bag and offered him a link of dried sausage. Upon seeing it, the man assured her that this gesture was unnecessary. But when the young wife insisted (insisted, mind you!), he accepted the sausage with his humble thanks and another doff of the cap.

Petya, who was now sitting as upright as a teacher's pet, watched the man in the cap get summoned by a woman farther back in the line. As she pointed this way and that, the man listened with apparent sympathy. Then, when he nodded his head, she darted off and he assumed her place without incident.

Petya ended up spending the rest of the day on the church's steps, and during those hours he saw the man in the cap go through the line three separate times on behalf of three separate women, receiving the link of sausage, a can of beans and two cups of sugar!

When at last the baker latched his door and the man headed home, Petya followed in hot pursuit.

'Hey, doffer,' he called.

Turning in some surprise, Pushkin looked down at the boy.

'Are you calling to me, young man?'

'You and nobody else. Listen. I've been around this town all my life. And I've seen my share of smooth-talking schemes. But what sort of racket is this?'

'Racket?' asked Pushkin.

With the narrowed eyes of the worldly, Petya was about to press his point when a fifty-year-old apparatchik approached out of breath. From the manner in which this fellow's belly strained against his vest, you could tell that his bread came buttered on both sides. Yet, he addressed the doffer with an unmistakable air of respect.

'Pushkin! Thank goodness! I was worried I might have missed you!'

Noticing Petya, Mr Bread-and-Butter put an arm over Pushkin's shoulders, turned him ninety degrees and continued in a lowered voice.

'I have it on good authority, my friend, that a shipment of electric lamps will be arriving in the illumination department of GUM tomorrow afternoon. Needless to say, I am in meetings most of the day. Do you think you might have time to hold a place for me until I can get there?'

Standing on his toes and leaning to his right, Petya could see that this Pushkin, who was listening with the utmost attention, was suddenly overcome with regret.

'Comrade Krakovitz, I am afraid that I have already promised Marya Borevna that I will stand in line for her at the butcher's while she is at Gastronome #4 getting figs in honor of her husband's name day.'

Krakovitz dropped his shoulders with such disappointment that he nearly burst his buttons. But when he turned to go, Petya piped up.

'Comrade Pushkin,' he said. 'Surely, we cannot afford to have the gentleman preparing for his meetings without the benefit of electric light! As your assistant, perhaps I could stand in line at the butcher's, while you stand in line at GUM.'

'Why, of course!' said Krakovitz, his face lighting up like the lamp he was hoping to procure. 'How about it, Pushkin?'

So, the very next day, while Pushkin waited at GUM, Petya waited at the butcher's shop. And when Marya Borevna came to assume her spot, as a token of her gratitude, she handed Petya a fistful of figs.

'How nice of Marya to share with you some of her fruit,' said Pushkin, when Petya came to GUM to give his report. 'You have certainly earned them, my boy.' But Petya would have none of that. He insisted that the two of them split the figs 50/50, on the grounds that while he had performed the labor, the business plan was Pushkin's.

Thus, it began. Within a week, Petya was standing in two or three lines a day, so that Pushkin could stand in two or three more. A professionally minded lad, Petya took pains to behave exactly as Pushkin would. That is, he never expressed the slightest impatience; rather, he remarked on the weather and the building across the street; he asked about progeny, either nodding his head in approval or shaking his head in sympathy as the circumstances demanded; and in parting, he always doffed his cap. In this manner, Petya was quickly accepted as Pushkin's proxy and he was welcomed just as warmly by all the women who waited.

8

If there is a terrain conducive to apple trees, within a few generations there will be all manner of apple trees growing branch to branch. If there is a neighborhood conducive to poetry, all manner of poets will soon be scribbling side by side. And so it was with the lines of Soviet Moscow. At any given moment, across the city could now be found lines for staples and lines for sundries. There were lines to board buses and lines to buy books. There were lines to obtain apartments, school placements and union memberships. In those years, if there was something worth having, it was worth standing in line for. But of all the various lines, the ones that Petya kept his closest eye on were the lines that served the elites.

As a younger man, Petya had assumed that there was no such thing. After all, wasn't that the whole point of climbing over the shoulders of your fellow men? To be free of the lines once and for all? But if the elites didn't need to stand in line to get what everyone else was waiting for, they had their *own* reasons to stand in line. They wanted bigger apartments. They wanted a car and driver. They wanted a fur coat for their mistress and a dacha on the outskirts of town.

One didn't have to read an annotated copy of *Das Kapital* to understand that those who wanted things of greater value were likely to express a greater sense of gratitude whenever their wishes came true. And since you can't break off a chunk of a dacha or divvy up a cashmere coat, the elites tended to show their gratitude in the form of cash – and often in foreign currencies!

But whatever their compositions – long or short, shy or shifty, fish or fowl – Moscow had more lines to stand in than Pushkin and Petya had feet. So Petya recruited a few of his fellows, and then a few more.

Such that by 1925, Pushkin had ten boys waiting in thirty lines, each of them handing tokens of gratitude up the chain of command.

9

The human race is notoriously adaptive, but there is nothing that a human will adapt to more quickly than an improved standard of living. Thus, while Irina had arrived in Moscow dedicated heart and soul to the upending of the social order – that is, to the defeat of the privileged and the victory of the proletariat – as the years unfolded, her understanding of how this might best be achieved evolved . . .

The evolution began, naturally enough, back in 1921 with that handful of candy sticks. When Pushkin had returned home with the cabbage in one hand and confections in the other, Irina was prepared to berate him from top to bottom for wasting hard-earned money on the fancies of a child. But when Pushkin explained how he had come by the candies, she was stymied. Her husband's willingness to wait in line for a mother-in-need seemed comradely to the core; and since he hadn't anticipated receiving the candies, one could hardly brand him a speculator. So, Irina decided to save her top-to-bottom for another day. And when Pushkin came home later that week with a sausage, after a moment's hesitation Irina nodded that this too was perfectly correct. After all, hadn't Lenin himself predicted that the successful transition to Communism would result in a little more sausage for us all?

As sausages evolved into cloaks and cloaks into cash, Irina began to recognize another achievement of Communism – through the transformation of her husband. For when they had lived in the country, Irina had always considered her husband to be a man without energy, intention or sense. But it had become increasingly clear that Pushkin had merely *seemed* that way. Once her husband had been freed by Bolshevism from the quasi-serfdom of the old regime, he had been revealed as a man of considerable talents; and not only did he help wives and widows obtain their necessities, he had virtually adopted a whole generation of orphans and turned them into productive citizens! So, with a touch of moral satisfaction, Irina allocated the sausages to the pantry, the cloaks to the closet and the cash to the bureau's bottom drawer.

Then one day in 1926, Comrade Krakovitz, who happened to be an undersecretary in the Department of Residential Accommodations, asked if Pushkin would wait in line for a case of French champagne. When Pushkin succeeded, Comrade Krakovitz was loath to show his appreciation by giving up a bottle; so, instead, with the stroke of a pen he reassigned Pushkin to a generous apartment in the Nikitsky Towers – a brand-new complex on the banks of the Moskva River.

Later that night, when Pushkin got home and explained to Irina what had happened, Irina soberly considered the turn of events. It was a common misconception – or so her thought process unfolded – that Communism guaranteed an identical life for all. What Communism actually guaranteed is that, in place of lineage and luck, the state would determine who should get what after taking careful account of the greater good. From this simple principle, it followed that a comrade who plays a greater role in attaining the greater good for the greater number of people should have greater resources at his own disposal. Just ask Nikolai Bukharin, editor of *Pravda* and champion of the peasant, who lived in a four-room suite at the Metropol Hotel!

Through this indisputable logic, Irina came to see their improved situation as the natural course of events; and she now often referred to Pushkin as 'comrade husband'.

10

Just as the poet in Pushkin's soul had once written odes to sprouting shoots and summer rain, he now turned his verses to pigeons that perched on pediments and trolleys that rattled in the lane. Which is to say, once again Pushkin's life with Irina was so satisfactory he wouldn't know what to wish for. That is, until 2 May 1929.

Earlier that week, the secret police had swept up five intellectuals and quickly convicted them of counterrevolutionary activities under Article 58 of the Criminal Code. Once these traitors were safely on their way to Siberia, a team was sent to their apartments with orders to gather up their books and deliver them to the municipal furnace. Now, it just so happens that as this disposal truck laden down with literature was taking a left onto Tverskaya Street at full speed, the centrifugal force from the turn sent one of the books flying at the very moment that our hero was about to step from the curb such that it spun twice in the air and landed at his feet.

As Pushkin wasn't much of a reader, he was about to step over the book and continue on his way, but something about it caught his eye. Bending over, he picked it off the ground. Then, having looked once to his left and once to his right, he tore off the cover and stuffed it in his pocket, having discarded the rest of the book.

Fifteen minutes later, when Pushkin arrived home, he called out to Irina. Hearing no reply, he went to their bedroom and closed the door. But realizing that he wouldn't hear his wife arrive if the bedroom door were closed, he opened it again. Then he sat on the bed and removed the book cover from his coat.

The book appeared to be in English, a language which Pushkin neither spoke nor read – so he was not intrigued by the title. What had caught Pushkin's eye was the black-and-white photograph that spanned the cover. It was a picture of a young woman lying on a chaise longue in a long white dress with a double strand of beads draped around her neck. Her hair was blonde, her eyebrows thin, and her lips delicate and dark. Simply put, she was the most beautiful woman that Pushkin had ever seen.

But she was not alone.

With an arm behind her head and a smile on her face, she was looking at a man who was seated with his back to the camera – a man in a tuxedo with a drink in his hand and a cigarette within reach.

For the first time in his life, Pushkin felt a pang of envy. It was not for the young couple's wealth that he felt envious, nor for the glamorous serenity that they seemed to be sharing on this terrace in the fabled city of New York. No. What made him envious was the smile that the beautiful young woman was directing toward her companion. In all Pushkin's life, he had never imagined being smiled upon in such a way by such a woman.

In the weeks that followed, when Pushkin got home he would sit on his bed with the door ajar, take the folded picture from his wallet and look at it anew. Often, he would notice something he hadn't noticed before – like the white roses that grew along the terrace, or the sparkling bracelet on the woman's wrist, or the high-heeled shoes on her slender feet. And late at night when he couldn't sleep, Pushkin found himself imagining that *he* was the man in the chair; that he was the man with a drink in his hand and a cigarette within reach, being smiled upon by this beautiful young woman in a dress of white.

11

Some months later, while Pushkin was waiting in line to buy a soup bone, he happened to be next to a gentleman in his late fifties by the name of Sergei Litvinov. After they had shared their views about the approach of autumn, the gentleman happened to remark that he worked at a local elementary school where he was responsible for sweeping the floors.

'Bless my soul,' exclaimed Pushkin. 'I too was once a sweeper of floors!'

'Were you, now?' said Litvinov with reciprocal enthusiasm. And as the two men discussed the differing aerodynamics of paper scraps and motes of flour the minutes went jogging along. But when Pushkin asked if the gentleman had always been a sweeper, Litvinov solemnly shook his head. It seems that in the decades before the war, Litvinov had been a portrait painter of some renown. In fact, two of his portraits had hung in the Tretyakov Gallery. But as he had primarily painted members of the aristocracy, in 1920 the Moscow Union of Artists had deemed him aesthetically unreliable and revoked his license to paint. Thus, to make ends meet, he had taken the job as a sweeper.

'After all,' said Litvinov with a smile, 'isn't a broom just a very large paintbrush?'

Pushkin had never been to the Tretyakov Gallery, or any museum for that matter. But he had knelt before many an icon in his day, and had always marveled at an artist's ability to render the human face in such convincing detail. To possess such a gift and no longer be allowed to put it to use struck Pushkin as heartbreaking and he could not help but ask if Litvinov felt some resentment.

Litvinov responded with another smile.

'I have lived under these circumstances for nine years, my friend. That is a long time to give one's life over to resentment.'

Then after a moment of reflection, Litvinov went on.

'My grandmother was fond of saying that whatever one chooses to do with one's life, one still must do one's part. And though the life of a painter may seem frivolous to some, whenever I would unveil a finished work before my subject and see their expression, I knew that I had fulfilled my grandmother's maxim. But you see, my friend, I was only half-kidding when I compared my paintbrush to my broom. For – perhaps to my own surprise – whenever I see the children running down the freshly swept hallways of the schoolhouse, I feel that once again I am doing my part.'

Though Pushkin was not familiar with the word *magnanimity*, he knew well enough that he was in its presence when he spoke to this painter-sweeper, such that upon parting, he shook Litvinov's hand with feelings of the deepest admiration.

But when Pushkin ran into Litvinov thirty days later, the gentleman looked like he had aged as many years. A parent, it seems, had filed a complaint with the District Educational Committee – that a painter of tsarist cronies should not be working in a schoolhouse filled with children. The next day, Litvinov's little apartment had been searched by the police, then he'd been taken to the Lubyanka, where he was held for three days of questioning. Though no charges were brought, upon Litvinov's return to the schoolhouse he was reprimanded by the headmaster for his absenteeism; the teachers who had been in the habit of chatting with him as he emptied their waste baskets, now remained silent; and worst of all, the students who had once returned his wave in the hallways, now averted their eyes.

'Back in '17, when my fellows folded their easels and fled to Paris, I shook my head. "Our calling is to paint the faces of our countrymen," I said, "with all of their whims and worries, all of their virtues and vices. What matters it to us, whether they wear grand mustaches or a pointed goatee?" So I said at the time, but now . . .'

Litvinov was quiet for a moment. Then, with a heavy heart, he acknowledged that while sweeping the floors, he had begun to daydream of standing in a railway station with an overnight bag in one hand and a bright yellow card in the other – a bright yellow card marked by a crimson stamp.

Pushkin's eyes grew wide.

'A stamp in the shape of St Basil's?'

'Yes,' admitted Litvinov with a hint of shame. 'From the Agency of Expatriate Affairs.'

Now, of all the lines in Moscow, the line that was the most elusive, the most daunting, the most insurmountable was the one that led to the Agency of Expatriate Affairs – that department in which one applied for an exit visa from Russia. Just finding the line was a challenge. For the agency's office was located deep within the Kremlin, up two and down three flights of stairs, at the end of a long series of lefts and rights, on a narrow corridor with forty doors that each looked alike.

Should you be lucky enough to navigate this maze and locate the office, once inside you were handed a pencil, a twenty-page form, and were directed to the back of the line. Naturally, the form requested your name, address, occupation and date of birth, along with your educational history, religious upbringing and social origin. But in addition, it required you to list the names, patronymics, diminutives and other endearments for all family members alongside their ages, sexes and professions; it required your history of ailments, infirmities and treatments; your involvements with the judicial system whether as a plaintiff, defendant or witness; the sources of your income and the sum of your savings; etc. At the conclusion of this exhaustive survey came the essay questions: *What is the country to which you want to travel? Have you ever traveled there before and why? For what purpose do you wish to travel there now? And, more to the point, why would you want to leave Russia in the first place!*

After waiting several days (which was just as well, since it took several days to fill out the form) you would reach the little window where you could submit your application. The clerk, in turn, would carefully grade it, taking into consideration your thoroughness, clarity and penmanship. Should the clerk award you a grade of D or F then, congratulations, your application was torn to shreds and you were sent to the back of the line. Should you be given a B or C, you would be handed a new pencil along with instructions of how to correct your submission – while everyone waited behind you. But were you one of the fortunate few who completed his application flawlessly on the very first go, you were ushered to an interior office where a caseworker sat behind a little metal desk with your application in hand.

Starting at the top, the caseworker would ask you every single question anew, presumably in search of discrepancies. At any point in the interview, the raise of an eyebrow or a truncated cough could signal that you were on your way back to the end of the line. But should you survive the interview, you would be asked to wait as your file was sent upstairs for consideration by an untold number of scrutineers. Only if every single one of them initialed the application to indicate they found no cause for concern would it circle its way back to the caseworker's desk, where it would receive that crimson stamp which opened, for a moment, the gates of the Soviet Union.

Though, naturally enough, most applications were refused, there were well-known stories of whole families making their way to Paris or London with the implicit blessing of the Politburo. But on what grounds these lucky few were allowed to leave remained a mystery. One citizen seemed to be granted passage on account of his spotless record as a Communist and his extended family in Berlin; while another was refused his visa *because* he was a spotless Communist with relatives in Berlin. Your visa could be stamped or rejected on the grounds that you were or were not a scientist, were or were not hard-working, were or were not a Jew. So unpredictable was the decision-making of the department that rumors circulated of a locked room in a sub-basement where ten colorful wheels like those in a carnival would be spun every morning to determine the ten criteria that on that day would result in the awarding of a visa!

'Yes,' admitted Litvinov with a hint of shame. 'From the Agency of Expatriate Affairs.'

Pushkin studied his new friend. 'If one cannot sweep in Moscow,' he said after a moment, 'then one should paint in Paris.'

Litvinov smiled in appreciation of Pushkin's support, but sadly shook his head.

'They say that waiting in that line can take weeks, and Headmaster Spitsky has made it perfectly clear that any further instances of "absenteeism" on my part will result in immediate dismissal . . .'

'I could stand in line for you.'

'Ah, my friend, you are too kind. But no one even knows where the line is.'

'I know exactly where it is. And besides,' Pushkin concluded with the utmost satisfaction, 'we all must do our part!'

12

The line at the Agency of Expatriate Affairs was quieter than any line in which Pushkin had ever waited. So anxious were those assembled that any effort at friendly conversation was immediately cut short by a frown. Thus, after three days of silence, Pushkin decided to fill out one of the agency's notorious forms simply to pass the time.

But what a delightful process it proved to be!

Without any desire to leave Russia, Pushkin felt no anxiety as to the political implications of his answers. Rather, he saw each question as an invitation to recall some heart-warming aspect of his past. Like his childhood in the village of Gogolitsky, where his older brother had taught him how to trap rabbits and where his mother would sing as she hung the laundry out to dry. But best of all was when it asked about his work experience. Here, Pushkin described how he and Irina would till their acres and harvest their harvest; and how in the lilac light they would journey home to their little table where the cabbage soup awaited. What wonderful years those had been! In fact, Pushkin had so many memories worth sharing that they spilled into the margins and wrapped around the page. And when he read the final question – *Why do you want to leave Russia?* – without hesitation, he answered: *I don't.*

After eighteen days of waiting in line, Pushkin called on Litvinov with the good news that he would reach the clerk's window on the following day by noon.

'Then I will be there at eight!' assured a grateful Litvinov.

But on the following day, Litvinov was not there at 8.00. He was not there at 9.00 or 10.00 or 11.00; and he was not there at 11.35 when the clerk at the window rang his little bell and called out, '*Next!*'

Unsure of what to do, Pushkin looked back at the door, but the citizen who was standing behind him gave him a shove and sent him stumbling toward the window.

'Come on, come on,' said the clerk. 'We haven't got all day. Give us your form.'

At that moment, Pushkin would have given the clerk Litvinov's form if he'd had it; but the painter-sweeper had kept it overnight in order to double-check his answers. So, with no other choice, Pushkin produced the form that he had filled out to pass the time.

When the clerk saw that Pushkin had folded the form down

the middle to fit in his pocket, he scowled. Laying it on the counter he made a great show of smoothing it open to indicate to all the applicants that the folding of forms was well out of bounds. Once the form was flat, he picked up his pencil and began reviewing Pushkin's answers, ready to pounce on the slightest error. But as he read, he found himself nodding in spite of himself; and when he reached the answer that wrapped around the page – a breach of protocol that would normally have guaranteed a shredding – the clerk let out a sigh. Not a sigh of exasperation, you understand, but a sigh of such sentimental satisfaction that he marked the passage with a star. But when the clerk reached the penultimate page, he looked up at Pushkin in surprise.

'You have not completed question 110.'

Pushkin looked down at the document as surprised as the clerk.

'Question 110?'

'Yes,' said the clerk. 'Where one indicates the place to which one wishes to go.'

Pushkin, who must have skipped the question in error, didn't know what to say, for he had never given it a moment's thought. With the clerk staring at him expectantly, Pushkin racked his brain. Irina, he seemed to remember, had always wanted to visit the Black Sea, but that was in Russia . . . The man who was next in line began audibly tapping his foot, which only made Pushkin's task more difficult. Then, suddenly, he thought of the lovely young woman in his wallet.

'New York City?' he suggested, tentatively.

Not only did the clerk offer no rebuke to Pushkin, he wrote the answer in the allotted space himself then waved Pushkin into an adjacent room. An hour or so later, a door opened and Pushkin was led not to the office of a caseworker, but to the director of the whole department. The director, who was a heavyset fellow with bags under his eyes, signaled that Pushkin should sit. In accordance with normal procedure, he was supposed to review Pushkin's form from the very beginning in search of oversights and discrepancies. Instead, he turned to the fourteenth page.

'Repeat for me, if you would, your history of work experience.'

Pushkin had not bothered to memorize the words he'd used in his answers, but he hadn't needed to – for he had memorized them with his life. So, he recounted to the director how he and Irina had tilled the soil row by row. He told of the crickets at twilight and the golden hues of harvest. And the director, who was raised among the wheat fields of Ukraine, wiped a tear from his eye with as unsentimental a knuckle as had ever been fashioned by God. Then, flipping back a few pages to where Pushkin had described his youth in Gogolitsky, the director spun the form around and tapped at a question.

'Here,' he said. 'Read this one.'

Then he leaned back in his chair and closed his eyes so that he could listen with greater care as Pushkin related his memories one by one.

Who knows what criteria the ten colorful wheels in the sub-basement of the Kremlin landed upon that morning after spinning round and round? But when Pushkin rose from his chair, he received a shake of the hand, a kiss on both cheeks and the stamp in the shape of St Basil's.

13

Not since that first day, when he had succeeded in getting bread and sugar but failed in getting milk, had Pushkin felt such trepidation at the sound of Irina's footsteps on the stair.

When she came through the door, she could tell at once that something was amiss. She could tell from the expression on her husband's face, from the shuffling of his feet and from the manner in which he asked about her day, which is to say, in triplicate.

'As I've told you twice already,' Irina replied, 'my day was productive. What about yours? And why are your hands behind your back?'

'Behind my back?' asked Pushkin. 'Well, yes, you see, earlier today, up two flights of stairs and down another three, at the end of a long series of lefts and rights, it just so happened, through no fault of my own –'

'Yes, yes?'

Then out spilled Pushkin's tale: of his friendship with Litvinov, the painter-sweeper, and the importance of doing one's part; of the unusual silence at the Agency of Expatriate Affairs and the filling of forms to pass the time with reference to crickets in the knee-high grass.

Irina was staring at her husband in confusion. Who was this Litvinov and what was a painter-sweeper? Which office was up and down, left and right? And what did crickets have to do with it?

Here, at a loss of what to add, Pushkin simply brought his hands from behind his back and held out the bright yellow card, which Irina snapped from his fingers. If Pushkin had feared the card would fill his wife with fury, he was not mistaken. When she saw typed across its top in capital letters the words REQUEST FOR A VISA, her cheeks grew red. When she saw her own name listed as one of the applicants, her ears grew red. And when she saw the requested destination identified as 'New York City', the blood that was boiling in her heart reached every single extremity. But even as the boiling blood raced through her veins, a series of thoughts raced through her head, holding her instinct to bludgeon her husband in check.

First, there was the reassessment of her husband's qualities. Once an aimless, unimaginative idler, he had proven to be the very personification of the Bolshevik ideal: tireless, single-minded and effective. So, like all good Bolsheviks, he deserved the benefit of the doubt. Then there was her deep-seated respect for the Kremlin's stamps. These were not tossed about like apples in an orchard. Whatever evidence to the contrary, the very appearance of such a stamp should confirm that a piece of paper had been carefully reviewed and deemed in perfect alignment with the Bolshevik cause. But to even consider leaving the Soviet Union so near its moment of triumph – and for New York City, no less – was this nothing more than the act of turncoat?

Rather than look to her husband for an answer, Irina looked to the portrait that was hanging on the wall. Returning her gaze with sober affection, the Father of the Revolution reminded her that the victory of the proletariat would come only once every worker of the world was united in the brotherhood of socialism. From the beginning, the

Bolsheviks' intention had been to establish a *foothold* in Russia and then expand the movement across the globe. And as to New York City, when a blacksmith hopes to shape a piece of iron, where better to thrust it than the center of the furnace?

'Very good,' Irina said as the blood withdrew from her fists. 'Very good, comrade husband.'

But having come to this conclusion through the soundest of reasoning, Irina suggested that they pack their clothes into one suitcase, their cash into another and leave without further delay. After all, Irina may have been a Bolshevik through and through, but she was no fool. And as if Fate itself wished to acknowledge the aptness of this instinct, when Irina and Pushkin emerged from their building with their suitcases in hand, they found a limousine idling at the curb.

14

In the years before the war, while working as a truck driver in Moscow, Maximilian Shaposhnikov had looked down upon the city's chauffeurs – finding their servile manners and silly black caps reason enough for his derision. But under Communism, he quickly discovered that the life of a chauffeur had its advantages. Specifically, if one was lucky enough to serve a vigilant member of the Party (the sort who routinely worked from dawn till dusk and sometimes through the night), then one had much of the day in which to use the boss's car as one saw fit. And in the new Russia, there was no shortage of black marketeers, prostitutes and other people of consequence who needed to get from point A to point B, who deserved to do so in style and who were willing to pay by the hour. Shaposhnikov had just dropped off one such client at the Nikitsky Towers when Pushkin and Irina came through the door.

Upon seeing the couple, Shaposhnikov didn't think twice. He donned his silly black cap and stepped from the car.

'Hey there, comrades,' he called. 'You look like you're off on a journey. Need a lift?'

Irina turned to her husband.

'Hire this fellow to take us to the station. I've forgotten something upstairs.'

While Irina went to retrieve the picture of Lenin that she'd left hanging on the wall, Pushkin explained to Shaposhnikov that they were, in fact, headed to the train station to catch a train.

'The overnight to Leningrad?'

'Why, yes.'

'For an extended visit?'

'No. We are actually going to Leningrad to catch the boat to Bremen and from there the steamer to New York.'

Maximilian Shaposhnikov may have been a man of Moscow, but he was also a man of the world. A couple living in the Nikitsky Towers heading to Bremen to catch a steamer for the States with two stuffed suitcases could only mean one thing – that the time had come to shear the sheep.

'Ah, the life at sea,' said Shaposhnikov with a nostalgic smile, though he'd never laid eyes upon it. 'Do you already have your tickets for the crossing . . . ?'

'I'm afraid we don't even have our tickets for the train.'

The chauffeur puffed out his chest and straightened his cap.

'Providence is smiling on you today, good sir. For I happen to know just the man to secure you a suitable carriage for the train ride to Leningrad and another to secure you a suitable cabin for your crossing.' Which was largely true! For from his days as a truck driver, Shaposhnikov had come to know a slew of fellows who now manned the docks and depots of Russia.

At the station, Shaposhnikov proved the perfect major-domo. He found Irina a comfortable seat and a cup of tea. He found a porter to take care of the bags. He introduced Pushkin to the ticket master (who would ensure that they had a first-rate berth in the sleeping car) and to the head conductor (who would ensure they had a first-rate table in the dining car). What's more, he contacted his friends in Leningrad to ensure that for their crossing to America they would be ticketed, portered and cabined in the first-rate manner by first-rate men. And at each juncture, Shaposhnikov gave Pushkin a little guidance on how best to show his gratitude to those who'd been of service.

Thus, with every step made smoother than the last, on 24 October 1929, Pushkin and Irina arrived in Bremen and climbed the gangplank. A horn was given three great blasts, confetti was showered over the docks, hats were waved at the rail and their steamship set out to sea – at the very moment that the stock market in the city of New York finally began its precipitous plunge.

15

Irina knew herself well. Not only did she know what she was capable of, she knew what she needed to do and when she needed to do it. What she did not know was that she was prone to seasickness. With the first swell of the ocean, it seemed as if a serpent had slithered into her stomach and now swam round and round. So, most of her Atlantic crossing was spent measuring the distance between the pillows on her bed and the porcelain in the water closet.

Pushkin offered to remain at Irina's bedside with a cold wet cloth. But knowing full well that her husband's constant attention would make the journey interminable, she pushed him out of their berth, insisting that he enjoy the freedoms of the ship from stem to stern. And despite his initial hesitations, that's exactly what Pushkin did.

Naturally, he enjoyed the endless vistas, and the four-course meals, and the jazz band in the bar. But what he enjoyed most of all was the ocean liner's staff. It seemed to Pushkin that for every passenger on board there were at least two members of the crew eager to ensure one's comfort. On the lower decks there were chambermaids, cabin boys and valets. In the dining room there were maître d's, waitresses and a fellow with a high white hat who carved the beef to order. While on the upper deck there were fine young men who would arrange your chair and fine young women who would bring your tea. And to his utter delight, Pushkin found that he had ample opportunity to show his appreciation to each and every one of them. Such that when Pushkin and his wife disembarked in New York at seven in the morning, they had no need of a porter because one of their suitcases was empty.

16

'**E** mpty!' exclaimed Irina, as she stood with her husband in the passenger terminal on the West Side piers. 'Empty!'

As Pushkin began to enumerate the many kind people who had shown their willingness to be of assistance over the course of the journey from Moscow to New York, she stared at him in amazement. In bewilderment. In disbelief. Who in his right mind would dole out a small fortune in hard-earned currency to a pack of gracious wolves on the doorsteps of a foreign country? Who?

But in a flash, Irina knew the answer: *The man she married. That's who!*

Oh, how sweet had been the notion that her husband had been transformed; that after decades of aimlessness, he had proved to be a man of purpose and imagination; and that her judgment in marrying him had not been so misguided, after all. A delicious notion, indeed. A sugar-dusted, chocolate-frosted, custard-filled pastry puff of a notion.

But surely such transformations are not unheard of, ventured a sympathetic little voice in the back of Irina's head. *Doesn't a man have the capacity to change?* By way of answer, Irina shouted at her husband, 'Does a fish grow feathers?' Then, without another word, she walked out the door.

'Does a tortoise grow tusks?' she could be heard calling out as she marched along the quay at her epiphanous pace. 'Does a butterfly grow a beard?' And so engaged was she in this menagerie of common sense that she barely paid heed to her surroundings as she passed under the tracks of an elevated train and entered the rough-hewn streets of the Lower West Side.

But when she reached the corner of Tenth Avenue and 16th Street, she came to a stop. A few strides ahead, a lone woman in shirtsleeves was leaning against a wall and smoking a cigarette while a crowd across the street milled in front of a loading-dock door. In a single glance, Irina recognized the people in the crowd. She recognized them from the ruggedness of their clothes and the determination on their faces. The only difference between this assembly and the factory workers in Moscow was that they appeared to come from every corner of the globe. In their number were Africans and Asians, Germans and Italians, Irishmen and Poles. Wondering what she had happened upon, Irina looked up and saw a billboard on the building's roof displaying a golden disk the size of the sun.

Suddenly, the loading door rolled up with a clatter to reveal a man in suspenders in the company of two armed guards. In unison, every member of the crowd began to shout and wave their hands. For a moment, the foreman looked them over, then he began to point.

'Him, her. Her, him . . .'

Those whom he singled out were waved inside by the guards – having been bestowed the privilege of doing a hard day's work – while the rest were left to swallow their disappointment just as they had swallowed their pride.

When the loading door came down with a bang, the woman in shirtsleeves was no longer leaning idly against the wall. Having tossed her cigarette into the street, she began thrusting a piece of paper in the hands of every worker who passed. Some of the workers glanced at the leaflet as they walked away, others stuffed it in a pocket, but most let it fall to the ground. When a gust of winter wind raced down the street, one of the leaflets was swept in the air and dropped at Irina's feet.

Irina couldn't read a word on the leaflet, but embedded right in the middle of the text, staring back with an expression at once determined and wise, was none other than Vladimir Ilich Lenin.

Irina scanned the departing sample of the world's citizens and, sure enough, there among them she spied two young women wearing the headscarves of home. Rushing across the street Irina called to them.

'Hey there! Sisters! Do you speak Russian?'

The two women stopped.

'We speak Russian.'

'I have just arrived in America. What is this place?'

'It is the National Biscuit Company,' replied one while the other simply pointed to the roof.

Gripping the leaflet in both hands, Irina watched the two women follow their fellows into the heart of the city. Then she looked up again at the giant sun of a biscuit that towered over the building and, suddenly, even though she was an atheist through and through, she knew exactly why God had brought her here.

17

B ut what of our old friend Pushkin?
When Irina walked out of the terminal he assumed that, having quickly gotten her bearings, she would head into the city, secure a new apartment and then come back, just as she had on their first day in Moscow. So, he waited. Given all the people moving about, Pushkin understood the important thing was to stay in the spot where Irina had left him, so that she could find him upon her return.

In the hours that followed, his fellow passengers gathered their luggage and greeted their families, the taxis came and went, the porters dispersed and the terminal emptied, but there was no sign of Irina. At one point, Pushkin thought he saw her on the quay looking about, as if unsure of where she was. 'Irina!' he called as he ran outside. 'Irina, Irina!' But when he took her by the shoulder, she turned out to be a stranger who just happened to dress like his wife. Disappointed, Pushkin returned to his waiting spot only to discover that one suitcase now remained where once there had been two – the empty one, of course.

Assuming that some weary traveler had picked up the wrong bag in error, Pushkin went back outside onto the quay where, in fact, he saw a man in a fedora walking away with what looked like his case.

'Excuse me,' shouted Pushkin, as the hatted man crossed a busy street. 'Excuse me!'

As the man didn't seem to hear, Pushkin waited for the traffic to

subside, then scrambled down the thoroughfare. When he reached the
first and second intersections, Pushkin could still see the hatted man
with his case walking up ahead; but when he reached the third, the
man was gone. Coming to a stop, Pushkin looked left and right, just
in time to see the hatted man, having crossed the intersecting avenue,
cut through an alley and turn a corner. So, as quick as he could,
Pushkin crossed, cut and turned – only to find himself suddenly
in the middle of Times Square, where the street signs flashed, the
subway rumbled, the automobiles blared and a thousand men raced
north and south, each sporting a fedora. Dashing up the boulevard in
a state of panic, Pushkin was suddenly plagued by second thoughts
and doubled back. But now, not only could Pushkin see no sign of
his case, he could see no sign of the alley that he'd emerged from. In
other words, he was lost.

Feeling the threat of a tear for the first time since his youth,
Pushkin tried to mimic the stoicism that his friend Litvinov would
have shown, then saying something about two flights up and three
flights down, he fell in step with the movement of the crowd.

Though in every single line of Moscow, Pushkin was known as
a man of the finest architectural sensibilities, as he proceeded down
Broadway he barely took note of a pediment. At Herald Square, he
took no notice of the skybridge that connected Gimbel's department
store to its annexe. At Madison Square, he took no notice of the
Flatiron Building with its whimsical shape. And when he entered
City Hall Park, at five o'clock in the evening, he took no notice of the
Woolworth Building, despite the fact that until quite recently it had
been the tallest building in the world!

What Pushkin did take note of, as he collapsed onto a bench, was
how cold and hungry he had become. While he had had the foresight
to bring a winter coat and scarf to America, both were still in his
suitcase; and while he had eaten a hearty breakfast on the ship, that
must have been twelve hours ago. As if in confirmation, a nearby
clock tower began to chime the hour of six.

Rubbing his hands together and pounding his feet on the flagstones in a half-hearted attempt to make himself warmer, Pushkin suddenly noticed that an old man in a threadbare coat on the bench across the way was trying to get his attention. Pointing in the direction of the clock tower, the man said something to Pushkin, then he pointed in the other direction.

'I'm afraid I don't understand,' said Pushkin with a mournful shake of the head. 'I don't speak a word of English.'

Seeming to understand the spirit of Pushkin's reply, the man nodded with a sympathetic smile. Then, rising from his bench, he pointed again in the opposite direction of the clock and signaled to Pushkin in a manner that clearly meant, *This way, my friend. Come along.*

Persuaded by the old man's smile, Pushkin began to follow him down Broadway. After they had walked a block the old man pointed ahead to the steeple of a church. Pushkin assumed that they were headed there to get out of the cold by attending an evening service. But when they arrived at the church, rather than enter the great carved doors, the old man led Pushkin around to the back. And there, as the darkness of fall shrouded Manhattan, they came upon twenty ragged men waiting patiently by the vestry door as a hint of chicken soup wafted gently through the air.

Without hesitation, Pushkin took his place at the end of the line. But even as he did so, he noticed that another man in a threadbare coat was emerging from a nearby alley. Catching the gentleman's eye, Pushkin gave him a friendly wave as if to say, *It's over here. This way, my friend*, and then he smiled. For while Pushkin was standing at the end of the line, he knew that when the new fellow arrived, it would no longer be the end of the line. In fact, it would no longer be the end of anything at all. ■

Nuar Alsadir

Quantum Displacement

The hover of the pole-hugger on the Q train
no light   gray morning dotted with rain
smell of paper bag wet from steam of egg
or bread   I am McDonald's sad   as prototypic
as a breakfast sandwich   the leads in a Haneke film
invariably called George & Anne   I don't want
to be a figure others lean their names into
the woman in the Wieners poem waiting
for the speaker to kiss on her mouth   kiss off
to that   & into the air   as the Violent Femmes
sang that summer when love & its likeness
infected us all with music & rage ^ My daughter
likes Hello Kitty even though *she has no mouth*
& always looks sad   It's more important   I tell her
to feel deeply than to be happy   *To be happy*
writes Cioran   *you must constantly bear in mind*
the miseries you've escaped   But wouldn't that mean
your miseries had caught up with you?
^ The quiet beauty of the commuter insists
on surface   as we head toward Stillwell Ave
where staying still conflates with staying well
Tell that to the cat   who laments being wheeled
into the unknown in a lightless bag   I catch
a whiff of Pond's as she passes   what hollow
would smell like if space had scent   Liz tells me
I am of soil   Becky old paperbacks   she

& her sisters   chalk chalk & chalk   Some thoughts
leave residue   are palimpsest   a sheet of paper
in a child's hands ^ *You are here*   my daughter
pointed   *in the fifth dimension*   then folding the paper
& here simultaneously   to a spot directly above
I get it   said her sister   *like when I'm reading & feel*
I'm the character   but know I'm myself at the same time
^ The man beside me twists his wedding band
like a Rubik's cube he cannot solve   The unconscious
warned Jung   will direct your life   if it's not
made conscious   & you will call it fate ^ The pencil
I used to stab the clog in the bathroom sink
slipped yellow to green stripes to eraser down
the drain ^ Are the deeper problems always
invisible? ^ Dora suffered inversely   from upward
displacement   what she felt or imagined   or Freud
imagined or felt in imagining her imaginings
the hard-on accompanying Herr K's embrace
morphing upbody to mouth   cough that both encoded
& expelled   as all good symptoms will ^ The oldest
impulse is of mouth   *I should like to eat this*   or *I should*
like to spit this out   Would Hello Kitty   & the woman
waiting   necessarily displace downward   *I should*
like to repress this instead? ^ Light radiates as we cross
the Manhattan Bridge   a lattice hexagon hangs
amidst a cramped street   perfectly balanced
like a benzene ring   I miss everything I've rebelled against
organic chemistry   the thought of a future   bridges
south & west of here ^ GPS locations rarely match up
to where you are   though the all caps feel   as they always do
intrusive   body made word   even Keats disturbed Fanny
Brawne with his *I took your letter last night to bed with me*
words made body & bedded   *your name on the sealing*

wax obliterated   negative displaceability ^ Is that a feminine
dilemma   wax obliterated or wane to survive? ^ My seat
faces the back of the train   the past   say the Aymara
is before you   what is already-known   behind
your back   borough you speed into but cannot see
^ Express trains prolong moments by way of trapped
odor   intensified sensation   vehicle of the Romantics
Coleridge would have loved the Q   the ride
might have done some good for Clare as well   *My friends*
forsake me like a memory lost   Staying still is no antidote
to loss   A pencil left to memorialize the moment
reading stopped cracks a book's spine   a lover's
back   memory a fault line   ring around we all
fall down ^ A moment in English is a point in time
other languages locate in space   *the moment in which*
or *where*   In wen   overcrowded time-city   the psyche
fold & fractals   entangles with every object of approach
The woman to my left rests her grief on me
generations ululate beneath her breath ^ *Every night*
my daughter bemoaned   *it's the same thing   dinner*
I   too   suffered early-onset ennui   Now I parallel
park downhill   eat daily biscuits of sorrow
& edge ^ *You become more yourself*   he said
kissing forth my mouth ^ Who will memorize
my dream song if it has no words?   Language
is a Bug Out Bob   squeeze here   & associations
pop in the elsewhere   quantum displacement
contact improv between dimensions ^ Why search
for a point if time is spatially extended?   Meaning
is more of a dance   until you try to understand it

*murmur
of feline
lamentation*

TLC
The Literary Consultancy

MANUSCRIPT ASSESSMENT AND EDITORIAL ADVICE SINCE 1996

Bridging the gap between writers and the publishing industry, TLC works worldwide to provide market-aware services to writers writing in English at all levels.

TLC EDITORIAL

- Detailed critical assessments and services by professional editors for writing at all stages of development, in all genres
- Links with publishers and agents, and advice on self-publishing

TLC MENTORING

- 12 months of one-to-one support
- Online or in person feedback
- Includes a full manuscript assessment

TLC EVENTS

- Literary events on Craft, Creativity, and Being a Writer

T 020 7324 2563

E info@literaryconsultancy.co.uk

W www.literaryconsultancy.co.uk

 The Literary Consultancy

 @TLCUK

LONGSHORE DRIFT

Julia Armfield

There are basking sharks in the upper layers of the water –
prehistoric things, nightmare-mouthed and harmless. Plankton-
eaters, the way all seeming monsters are. They fill the coastal waters
in the summertime, rising up to trawl the krill blooms. Puckered with
barnacles, blasé as window-shoppers, they can grow over a lifetime
to twenty feet in length.

There are warning flags along the wrack line: SHARKS – SWIM AT
YOUR OWN RISK. The threat is actually minimal, basking sharks being
liable to give you little more than a bump on the knee, but the effect of
the signs is still an odd one. There are no barriers, the water is open,
creating the sense of a curiously lackadaisical approach to public
safety. *Danger, but do what you want, we're not the police.*

Around the rock pools, paddleboarders nudge the backs of sharks
with oars and suffer no retaliation. Mackerel fishers follow the oily cut
of dorsal fins, heading home with lockboxes full of tiddlers, waxing
mythical about the one that got away. Tall tales abound, swimmers
reimagine close calls and teeth where none existed. A story that seems
to crop up every year sees a woman snorkelling for sea glass swimming
right down into the open mouth of a basker, where she has a good look
at the contents of its stomach before coming out again, unscathed.
Ridiculous, of course, but in truth about as likely as anything else.

O n the beach, Alice turns the truck at the wooden groyne which marks the end of the so-called *pleasure section* and idles the engine, considering the view. The afternoon has been bad, toothy with chill, no one buying much.

'Six Fabs and a Mint Cornetto,' Min recites, checking seven items off on her fingers. 'Slim pickings, Captain.'

'It's the weather,' Alice replies, gesturing at the window to encompass the wanness of the day. 'Who wants an ice cream in a funk like this?'

The afternoon is only an attempt at itself – fretful greyness, minnow stink of gutweed. Overhead, the vulture wheel of hunting gulls, a white-lipped, murderous sky. At the wheel, Alice squints towards the headland, the tidal band of beached sargassum running out before her like the rising of some long-backed creature from the sand. In the back, perched on some stacked boxes of Cadbury Flakes, Min kicks her leg reflexively against the wall. 'Bummer,' she nods, pulling a serious face but snorting when Alice glances back at her. 'Bummerama. What are you staring at? Don't act like you're not impressed by my urban vernacular.'

'You talk such shit.'

Alice finds she says this a lot, usually while smiling. Min laughs. Lit by the neon glow of the Polar slush machine, she is like something pulled from ice. Alice can imagine her, defrosted and on show in a museum – an artefact preserved for history, academics pointing to the places on her body where the cold has marked her, the diamond stud in her nose.

'*That girl is headed nowhere,*' Alice's mother likes to say. Going over the house with a Hoover after Min leaves, '*I don't know why she has to be here every hour of the day.*'

Her objections are routine: Min's tacky nylon glamour, the street where she lives, the father who won't get out of bed. Her hair is bleach-fried, wilting in natural light. In the presence of Alice's mother, she has a nervous habit of fluffing it out like a mammal inflating its fur.

'*You're such a clever girl,*' Alice's mother will say whenever Min has just departed. '*Can't you find a cleverer sort of friend?*'

At school Alice is streamed into all the hardest sets, and it seems that the friendships she is expected to cultivate are also the hardest and dullest, the ones that come with the most supplementary work. Last year, she had been involved in a punishing sort of best-friendship with a girl named Pam who had won several prizes for debating, and talked droningly about *their relationship* as though they were husband and wife. They had spent their Friday evenings locked in a revolve of interminable sleepovers, Pam insisting they watched movies of her choice and then talking over them. If Pam stayed over at Alice's, she would mention all the things it was a shame they couldn't do that evening: it was a shame Alice didn't have Sky or a real computer, it was a shame Alice's mother only made normal toast, unlike Pam's mother, who made it French. By the end of term, Alice had started hanging around with Min after art class, and it was only via a protracted period of passive cruelty that Pam, waiting doggedly for Alice outside the science laboratories or at the back gates at four o'clock, had finally been shaken off. These days, Alice only sees her occasionally, hanging around with another girl named Karen, who is apparently a big deal in choir.

In the back of the truck, Min pushes herself upright, clambering forwards over the gearstick and into the passenger seat, giving Alice a chuck to the head as she goes. Her silver hair is straggled back into a ponytail, acid bunch behind her ears.

'Cut our losses, I would,' she says, chewing gum and planting her feet on the dashboard. 'Take her on a victory lap and then get out of here.'

'Victory how?' Alice grumbles. 'Six Fabs and a Mint Cornetto does not a victory make.'

'Cheer up, honey pie,' Min rubs her hands vigorously on her polyester shorts before leaning over to touch Alice's cheek. A jolt of electricity. 'Magic finger.' Min laughs and Alice wriggles away from her, jerking the clutch into first.

The music starts automatically, the ice-cream jingle, 'Que Sera Sera' on imitation chimes. Gulls scatter as the truck eases forwards, trundling towards higher ground. The tourists, for the most part, tend to keep to the safety of the dunes, bracketed behind canvas windbreakers, hunkered grimly over sandwiches and picking sand from the spines of overambitious holiday books. Every year, the coastguard finds on average six copies of *Anna Karenina* abandoned on the flats between April and high summer. The council has plans for a small exhibition.

Alice aims the truck inland, a crunching movement rumbling through the fabric of her skirt. Plastic cups and discarded tennis balls everywhere, cigarette butts stamped down and forming shapes like lugworm burrows in the sand. Manoeuvring up towards the dunes, Alice notes a bright scrim of shiny paper – a crumpled Fab wrapper – and feels momentarily guilty. The back doors of the truck are panelled with warning signs, painted on by Min's uncle in thick black bitumen: LITTER MAKES THE FUTURE BITTER; KEEP IT NICE, DON'T DROP YOUR ICE.

Wondering whether she ought to stop and scoop up the wrapper, Alice glances at Min, only to find her bunching up her chewing gum in a paper napkin, preparing to throw it out of the window.

'Oh, don't,' Alice says, regretting it almost immediately – the mumsy tone. Min raises an eyebrow at her, though she does withdraw her hand from the open window, throwing the napkin instead in the cupholder beside the gearstick.

'Fair enough,' she nods, and while her tone is light Alice feels she can detect the faintest note of mockery. 'Mustn't be bitter with my litter.'

It can be like this, sometimes. A sudden quirk of the lip. Alice biting back the wrong words. Sitting together in History, passing notes until Alice writes something stupid or uncool, underlines the wrong thing, and Min crumples the note in her fist.

'*Fair enough*', this stock phrase, its cringing detachment. The sudden removal of camaraderie and Alice clawing after it.

Alice opens her mouth to speak, but Min is now gesturing ahead to a group of teenaged boys who have wandered down from the slate flats that border the bank of seagrass. They are flagging down the truck. 'Thank fuck,' she exclaims. 'Passing trade. Pull up.'

Alice squints through the windscreen. The boys are their age or a little older. Of the group, three are in swimming trunks and two in wetsuits, all of them clutching preposterously at surfboards which collide as they approach the truck. The sea is still as pondwater.

'What are they going to do,' Alice grumbles as she brings the truck to a standstill. 'Build a fort with those things?'

'Who cares?' Min is already clambering back over the gearstick into the back section, sliding up the serving window and leaning almost all the way out. 'Well, aren't you boys a sight for sore eyes?'

The boys cluster like geese. One of them, wet-lipped with a tongue piercing, asks Min what she's doing selling ice cream on such a chilly day. *What's a nice girl like you doing in a truck like this.* Min's reply comes out static with the same electricity she discharged against Alice's cheek.

'Well, what are you doing *buying* ice cream on such a chilly day?'

Over her shoulder, Alice sees her friend as though beheaded; green shorts and a silver thread in her sweater, leaning elbows on the serving ledge, resting her chest on her folded hands. Her legs are coarse as soap and chicken-skinned with a two-day growth of hair. At the back of one knee she has a small tattoo, a Russian doll with its top removed and another, smaller face peeking out. Alice was with her when she got it, held her hand and watched the anxious sweat soak into the back of her T-shirt. *I contain multitudes* – the tattoo seems to say – *or at least five or six.* Afterwards, the two of them had gone for burgers, Min with her bandaged leg elevated and her foot on Alice's knee. Smearing ketchup, sharing a lemonade, Min leaning over to lick a daub of mustard off Alice's wrist. They had wandered up to the arcade at the end of the pier and Alice had spent all her money buying them games on the *Mortal Kombat* machine until Min had decided she was sick of playing because none of the female characters ever won.

A lice doesn't realise she is scowling until she catches her expression in the rear-view mirror. The boy with the tongue piercing is talking, brassy glint of unprecious metal, and Min's laugh is the same upside-down thing it always seems. He is asking whether the truck belongs to her and she is weaving him a series of stories: *her family inheritance; driven it from one end of this country to the other; the things you see from a serving hatch, you wouldn't believe.*

'She can't drive,' Alice wants to call over her shoulder. 'Her uncle did his knee in playing five-a-side and she's roped me into driving his truck because I passed my test.'

'Because she knew I'd have nothing better to do,' she also wants to call over her shoulder.

'I don't know what I want,' the boy with the tongue piercing is saying now, in a voice which fairly communicates that what he wants is probably not included on the menu. The serving side of the truck is panelled with pictured offerings in frantic technicolor; Zooms and Magnums and Soleros, pre-packaged ice-cream sandwiches on which Alice has experimented, leaving them out on paper plates for hours, coming back slightly disconcerted to find that they have failed to melt.

At the window, Min hangs even more precariously outwards, shifting sideways in a way which suggests she might be pointing at some item on the menu.

'Take your pick – little bit of what you fancy,' she says in her Mae West leer.

'How about you surprise me,' the tongue-pierced boy replies, and his friends chortle in a weird tandem. There is a sudden, queasy rocking of the truck, as though several people have leant up against it at once.

'Earl Grey and sardine ice cream it is,' Min replies, and Alice grins despite herself. It is a sleepover game they play, dreaming up the most disgusting of possible flavour combinations: lemon curd and spare ribs, duck and Parma Violets, tinned pilchards and strawberry jam. A strange pretence at early teenhood, despite the fact that they are both nearly eighteen – nights spent sleeping top to tail in Alice's bedroom and playing stupid games, inking outlines of the constellations on one another's arms in biro, tweezing eyebrows and talking on and on about kissing, Min's little moonstone teeth in the dark.

At the serving hatch, Min hooks one bony ankle over the other and Alice wills her to retract her head and wink at her, give some sign that they still share ownership of the joke she has just hurled unthinkingly away from them. But Min remains where she is and the joke sails away over the head of the boy whose fingers now appear on the edge of the hatch.

'Whatever sounds good to you,' he says. 'What's your name, anyway?'

Min draws back a little, though only to open up the chest freezer and root around inside.

'Minerva.'

'You're sweet, Minerva.'

Min snorts, kicking back one leg as though the knee has just been swiped out from under her.

'Nah, you're just all hot at the thought of ice cream.'

She hands something over – bright red wrapper – and there is a renewed sound of butting surfboards.

'What's this?' the boy with the tongue piercing asks, an anticipatory tone which has no business being used for ice cream.

'Your heart's desire.'

'You reckon?'

Min laughs.

'Good going for two quid, yeah?'

Alice has no enthusiasm for boys, except as they appear in the abstract – the fictional approximations that people the books she reads, appealing only in silhouette and with the meat cut out of their middles. In reality, boys appear to her like plane trees in a photograph, sudden and ugly and always just in the centre of things, giving idiotic answers in class and telling boring stories about how drunk they got the night before. Exactly where this distaste springs from is unclear to her. She isn't gay – she's pretty sure. She's tested it, stared at the women in her brother's magazines. In truth, it is something she thinks about only seldom, usually as an afterthought to the late-night recollection of old humiliations – the time Toby Waters had been moved next to her as punishment for talking in English class and had told everybody afterwards that she smelled; the time she announced to a group of friends that her favourite character in *Grease* was Marty when everyone else was saying Danny; the way a girl in sixth form had once looked her over and told her, apropos of nothing, that she had a straight girl's way of doing her hair.

She has only been kissed once, by the stock boy at the cafe where she worked for most of the previous summer; a nineteen-year-old with a shining ham of a face, who ate egg-salad sandwiches on his lunch breaks and sweated dark crescents into the armpits of his shirts. He had trapped her on the galley steps that led down to the meat freezer one day when she was running back to fetch something, bracketing her head against the wall and telling her how cute she was. His smell like egg and perspiration, soft sour note of Glacier Mints and his teeth too big and scraping against her own. She had let him do it, and afterwards slid into the meat freezer and stood there wondering what it was she had come to fetch.

Min likes boys, although always the wrong ones, too loud, bad-smelling or encumbered with long-term girlfriends. She is the kind of girl stitched together by brief liaisons – '*Bad-news girl*,' Alice's mother says in her hands-up church voice, '*shakes herself out like sheets.*' In the wind-down days of the summer term just gone, Min had dragged Alice out almost every weekend to a seafront bar bizarrely named the Credenza, where they had flashed their fake IDs at an indifferent bouncer and danced until Min found a boy to kiss. On the dance floor, a chalk-smeared stretch of glittering malachite, they would shimmy to nineties music, Min's hair lit up like a chemical spill by the disco lights. Most of the time the boys came easily, sloping over the way one approaches a dangerous dog, wary but still irrationally keen to touch. Occasionally, when the music was sluggish and the attention not forthcoming, Min would loop her arms around Alice's shoulders and angle down through her hips, winking solemnly as she did so, a complicit little change of rhythm. This never failed. The boys were usually ones they knew from school, although sometimes there were tourists or boys from inland towns down for the weekend surf. Min would disappear with whoever approached first for half an hour to forty-five minutes, emerging always smeared and alone to find Alice drinking fizzy water, grabbing her hand and demanding that they leave. She would give these boys a phone number when they asked for it, though it would always be Alice's number rather than her own.

'*It's like you're my protector*,' she would say, after Alice had spent another Saturday morning fending off calls from boys with names like Gus and Sam and Timbo, '*fighting off the vagabonds who would do me wrong.*'

By the end of term, Alice had perfected a fair approximation of Min's voice, brushing off the boys who called her up less delicately than she would care to admit. *It was a kiss – move on. I have herpes. I'm in love with the girl you saw me dancing with before.*

A t the serving hatch, Min is handing out Cornettos in a wide circle; clattering of surfboards like a racket of seagulls being fed.

'Calm down,' she says, clearly enjoying herself, 'plenty to go round.'

'Animals,' the boy with the tongue piercing agrees, prompting a grumble of insult from his companions. 'Grabbing at a girl like that.'

'Grabbing I can handle,' Min replies, and Alice finds herself rolling her eyes. The dispiriting sight of herself in the rear-view mirror, bad-tempered and raw with acne. She has never been very keen on the thought of herself as other people see her. The small lapine eyes, too far apart by several inches, the angry skin and colourless hair. Min likes to say she has a Georgian look to her, cutting black dots and stars out of sticky paper and patching her face with them. *There you go, blemish-free and oh-so-stylish.*

'Who else've you got back there?'

The question is sudden, the boy with the tongue piercing bracing his fingers against the serving hatch as though about to climb inside. Min glances back at Alice.

'Just my friend.'

'Just your friend?'

'Just my friend Alice.'

'Is Alice as sweet as you?'

A laugh. A boy comes round to the passenger-side window, pressing his face to the glass. Another boy joining him, and another. Gawping aquarium faces. Alice hooks her legs under her and looks over her shoulder at Min, who has turned back to the hatch.

'No, not as sweet as me.'

The boy with the tongue piercing laughs.

'So it's Sweet Mol –'

'Minerva.'

'Sweet Minerva and Savoury Alice.'

'That's what they call us.'

The day is darkening, growing soft about its edges. A rise in the wind has resulted in a minor improvement of the water, the waves now rolling at a choppy half-speed that has surfers picking their uncertain way down from the dunes. The boys around the truck seem collectively to notice this, sudden loosened pressure as they peel back from the windows to stare out to sea. A minor commotion. One of them has knocked against another and dropped his Cornetto. From the back of the truck, Min gives a high little laugh, but the attention trained on her moments before is distracted.

The boys are suddenly fractious, eager to be off. The one with the tongue piercing pulls his fingers from the hatch and Alice twists in her seat.

'He hasn't paid,' she says, not quite knowing if she means him to hear her. Min springs forwards through the hatch again.

'Wait a minute, this isn't a free dispensary – that's fifteen quid in total, thank you very much!' Her tone is irritatingly sweet, and the nonchalant reply only makes it worse.

'No money – nowhere to keep it in this get-up.'

Min retracts her head, white hair bristling at the nape of her neck, and Alice briefly envisages herself muscling up from the driver's seat and demanding the money.

'Tell you what though,' the boy with the tongue piercing continues, 'once we're done on the water we're going to get cleaned up and go into town. I'll have money then.'

'Not a lot of use to me now, is it?'

'No but it'll keep until I buy you a drink.'

The wind is coming in from the headland, pushing the ocean current sideways. Along the beach, Alice can see little tumbleweeds of silt and litter being blown across the sands, as though the beach has been tipped upwards at one corner and is leaking to the left. This gradual slip is one that has been going on for some years, a perpendicular drift of sediment caused by the swash and backwash of water on the beach. The wooden groynes that punctate the sands were set up only recently as a defence against this redistribution, though every year it still seems that a little more of the beach trickles gently off the surface of the map.

The boys move off in a pack, handprint smears of ice cream visible at the edges of their surfboards. Behind her, Alice hears Min slide the serving hatch shut. She puts the truck into gear without thinking about it and jerks the vehicle forwards, and Min stumbles against the freezer as she does.

'Hey, wait!'

The red flags along the wrack line beat out as if in semaphore, furling and unfurling in the breeze. Alice idles the van, waiting for Min to clamber up into the passenger seat, which she does with another chuck to Alice's chin. 'Safety first, Captain,' she says, ostentatiously drawing her seat belt across and grinning. She is happy again, though Alice's mood has darkened.

A hard sugar smell of freezer burn – dark smell, sweetness on the turn. Min kicks her feet up onto the dashboard and Alice finds herself irritated by her peeling toenail polish.

She looks at Min's arm, where the boy with the tongue piercing has scrawled a phone number. She wonders how he could have had a pen on him and claim to have nowhere to keep his change.

'He didn't pay,' she says again, squinting unnecessarily out of the front windscreen as she moves the truck forwards, as though trying to see her way through fog. The automatic chimes have started up again with the motion of the engine; 'Beautiful Dreamer' this time.

Min takes up the ball of paper in which she had previously wadded her gum and drops it out of the open window.

'We'll get it back.'

'What, when we go for a drink?'

Min leans her head forwards, fluffs out her hair.

'Exactly.'

'Pretty sure it was just you he was inviting.'

'Oh, Alice,' Min sighs, a voice that affects a weary maternal timbre; Alice's mother telling her to for God's sake stop picking her spots. *You're only making it worse.* 'If that's what you want to believe then I really can't help you. People don't issue exclusive invitations to drinks. He didn't call me up to the country club. Come or don't come, I don't know. Whatever you like. No one's going to care.'

The day is collapsing, soft deflation in the surface of the sky. Along the dunes, most of the tourists who have not already scuttled down to the sea are packing themselves away, hauling windbreakers inwards like sails to be stowed, throwing up the crusts of white-bread sandwiches to be caught mid-air by gulls.

'Best pack it in now, anyway,' Min is saying, and Alice finds herself scowling despite the logic of the statement. The ice-cream jingle has taken on a slightly unsettling tone with the threat of worsening weather – an eerie juxtaposition, the way wind chimes acquire a warning quality before a storm.

'Six Fabs and a Mint Cornetto.' Alice shrugs one shoulder, aiming the truck back up towards the concrete strip that leads into the upper car park. 'Your uncle's truck, your uncle's takings, not mine.'

'And fifteen quid's worth of ice cream just then!'

'Yes, well.'

'Yes, well to my unique powers of salesmanship!'

'Yes, well, all big business is run on the strength of IOUs.'

'All right, crabby.' Min leans back against the window, grinning slightly and moving one foot from the dashboard to prod at Alice's arm. Alice shrugs her off but Min persists, giggling as she moves her foot to again prod Alice's elbow, moving up in increments to tickle her shoulder, then her ear.

'*Stop it*,' Alice snaps without really expecting to, slapping at Min's foot until she removes it, her smile fading.

'Fair enough,' she shrugs, sitting back and slinking her feet beneath her.

A long the dunes that teeter from the upper car park, a blanket of glasswort creeps down towards the path. It is a samphire, of sorts, a prickled matting plant that grows in saline conditions and can, if burnt, yield soda and potash. Min's mother, on good days, sends her out to pull up handfuls of the stuff which she pickles in malted vinegar or renders into squat little soaps. These, in turn, she sells on Saturdays at coastal marketplaces, enlisting Min to lug them to and from the car, or to accost strangers and use her tight, acidic influence to persuade them to a purchase. Alice has accompanied Min once or twice on her harvesting trips, pulling up the sharp little branches more or less solo as Min sits higher up the flats and complains about her parents. '*Let her get an assistant*,' she'll say, watching Alice pulling weeds with little sense of irony. '*Let him get out of bed every once in a while and help her. What am I doing all this for, hey?*'

They had come down, once, at the very start of summer, tipsy after Min had got them forcibly ejected from the Credenza for yanking a bottle of Grolsch from behind the bar. They had managed to get away with the bottle and had skidded down the dunes in unsuitable shoes to drink it lying in the glasswort, each complaining at the spiny leaves creeping up beneath their skirts. Min, blue-lipsticked in a bluer twilight, had rambled on about a boy at the club who had ignored her, despite the fact that only two days previously she had allowed him to finger her behind the Hope and Anchor way out along the pier. Lying slightly sideways, Alice had stared down at the wooden groyne stretching out towards the water and had registered a curious sensation of slippage, a drifting down of all the bits and pieces of her body like a sloughing off of sand. Beside her, Min had smelled of beer and peanut brittle, a squeeze of Dior Poison from the big bottle Alice knew her mother kept in her desk.

'Next week I'll take you to a *proper* club,' Min had said – something she was always saying. 'We'll go somewhere where the men are *adults*. I'll buy you a martini in a proper glass.'

Her teeth had been unnaturally white, like pieces of the moon, and Alice had rolled her shoulders and said nothing.

'I *will*,' Min had said, apparently goaded by her silence. 'We'll do all sort of things this summer. Find you a boy for once. World's our oyster.'

She had caught Alice's wrist between her fingers in the casual, trickling way she liked to touch – slotting her arms around Alice's neck or looping fingers over fingers, jewellery gestures, beading and bangling and always too loose.

'World's our oyster,' she had repeated, and her lips had been electric blue and too bizarre to kiss.

M in had dragged her down to the water that night, Alice's wrist still shackled between finger and thumb as they bolted down beyond the wrack line. At the edge of the water, Min kicked off her shoes but pulled Alice in without waiting for her to remove her own. She had lost them almost immediately, carried off with the first white heave of water the way so many things seemed subject to this endless sideways shift. In the dark the warning flags were grey, the clouds glassy and colour-blind. They had aimed for the headland, kicking, an unobtrusive blackened current. Alice had ducked her head and let her body rise, held up by clothes that tentacled around her ankles as Min dragged her further out.

There were sharks in the shallows – baskers, harmless. A few hundred feet from the shore, Alice had felt Min's fingers release her and, grasping after her, had tipped her head beneath the water, caught her legs in the tangle of her dress and very suddenly sunk. Alice had found one there, only feet beneath her. They are vast things, baskers, whale-mouthed – filtering their food through a cavernous yawn of jaw not unlike the drum of a washing machine. A wave passing over her head, Alice had sunk further than expected, scrambling with the sudden weight of her clothes as the shark filled her frame of vision. The great mouth had seemed toothless, ribbed with bone, a mouth that she momentarily looked down, feeling briefly convinced, in her drowning confusion, that she could see everything from its guts and gullet to the small internal secret of its heart. The shark, for its part, had seemed unbothered by her presence, only tilting slightly to avoid her as she struggled, bumping by her the way one small boat might pass another in the night. Twisting sideways and thrashing her legs away from her dress, she briefly panicked, until a hand again enclosed her wrist and dragged her upwards, Min laughing in her face as she crested the surface, flinging arms in blind confusion round her neck.

'I thought you'd gone,' Alice had choked, and Min only rolled her eyes, treading water, her hair a glowstick crackle in the dark.

'Where would I go?' Min had deadpanned. 'Pubs'll be shut by now.'

Beneath her, Alice had felt the bump of fins beneath her feet and drew her legs up, briefly allowing Min to keep them both afloat. Some way off, before the shadow of the headland, the pier, ghostly in the way that all piers are, shimmered unobtrusively in sea-light. ∎

CHARLIE PARKER
PLAYS BOSSA NOVA

Haruki Murakami

TRANSLATED FROM THE JAPANESE BY PHILIP GABRIEL

B *ird is back.*

How fantastic that sounds! Yes indeed, the Bird you know and love has returned, his powerful wings beating the air. In every corner of this planet – from Novosibirsk to Timbuktu – people are going to gaze up at the sky, spy the shadow of that magnificent Bird and cheer. And the world will be filled once more with radiant sunlight.

The time is 1963. Years since people last heard the name Charlie 'Bird' Parker. Where is Bird, and what is he up to? Jazz lovers around the world whisper these questions. He can't be dead yet, can he? Because we never heard about him passing away. But you know, someone might say, I haven't heard anything about him still being alive either.

The last news anyone had about Bird was that he had been taken into the mansion of his patron, Baroness Nica, where he was battling various ailments. Jazz fans are well aware that Bird is a junkie. Heroin – that deadly, pure white powder. Rumor had it that on top of his addiction he was struggling with acute pneumonia, a variety of internal maladies, the symptoms of diabetes and even mental illness. If he was fortunate enough to survive all this, he must have been too infirm to ever pick up his instrument again. That's how Bird vanished from sight, transforming into a beautiful jazz legend. Around the year 1955.

Fast forward to the summer of 1963. Charlie Parker picks up his alto sax again and records an album in a studio outside of New York. And that album's title is Charlie Parker Plays Bossa Nova*!*

Can you believe it?

You'd better. Because it happened.

It really did.

This was the opening of a piece I wrote back in college. It was the first time that anything I wrote got published, and the first time I was paid a fee for something I'd written, though it was only a pittance.

Naturally, there's no such record as *Charlie Parker Plays Bossa Nova*. Charlie Parker passed away on 12 March 1955, and it wasn't until 1962 that bossa nova broke through, spurred on by performances by Stan Getz and others. But *if* Bird had survived until the 1960s, and *if* he had become interested in bossa nova and performed it . . . That was the setup for the review I wrote about this imaginary record.

The editor of the literary magazine at the university who published this article never doubted it was an actual album and ran it as an ordinary piece of music criticism. The editor's younger brother, a friend of mine, sold him on it, telling him I'd written some good stuff and that they should use my work. (The magazine folded after four issues. My review was in issue no. 3.)

A precious tape that Charlie Parker left behind had been discovered by accident in the vaults of a record company and had only recently seen the light of day – that was the premise I cooked up for the article. Maybe I shouldn't be the one to judge, but I still think this story is plausible in all its details, and the writing has real punch. So much so that in the end I nearly came to believe that the record actually existed.

There was considerable reaction to my article when the magazine published it. This was a small, low-key college journal, generally ignored. But there seemed to be quite a few readers who still idolized

Charlie Parker, and the editor received a series of letters complaining about my *moronic joke* and *thoughtless sacrilege*. Do other people lack a sense of humor? Or is my sense of humor kind of twisted? Hard to say. Some people apparently took the article at face value and even went to record shops in search of the album.

The editor kicked up a bit of a fuss about my tricking him. I didn't actually lie to him, but merely omitted a detailed explanation. He must have been secretly pleased that the article got so much attention, even though most of it was negative. Proof of that came when he told me he'd like to see whatever else I wrote, criticism or original work. (The magazine disappeared before I could show him another piece.)

My article went on as follows:

. . . Who would ever have imagined a lineup as unusual as this – Charlie Parker and Antônio Carlos Jobim joining forces? Jimmy Raney on guitar, Jobim on piano, Jimmy Garrison on bass, Roy Haynes on drums – a dream rhythm section so amazing it makes your heart pound just hearing the names. And on alto sax – who else but Charlie 'Bird' Parker.

Here are the names of the tracks:

> *Side A*
> *(1) Corcovado*
> *(2) Once I Loved (O Amor em Paz)*
> *(3) Just Friends*
> *(4) Bye Bye Blues (Chega de Saudade)*
>
> *Side B*
> *(1) Out of Nowhere*
> *(2) How Insensitive (Insensatez)*
> *(3) Once Again (Outra Vez)*
> *(4) Dindi*

*

With the exception of 'Just Friends' and 'Out of Nowhere' these are all well-known pieces composed by Jobim. The two pieces not by Jobim are both standards familiar from Parker's early, magnificent performances, though of course here they are done in a bossa nova rhythm, a totally new style. (And on these two pieces only the pianist wasn't Jobim but the versatile veteran Hank Jones.)

So, lover of jazz that you are, what's your first reaction when you hear the title Charlie Parker Plays Bossa Nova? *A yelp of surprise, I would imagine, followed close on by feelings of curiosity and anticipation. But soon wariness must raise its head – like ominous dark clouds appearing on what had been a beautiful, sunny hillside.*

Hold on just a minute. Are you telling me that Bird – Charlie Parker – is actually playing bossa nova? Seriously? Did Bird himself really want to play that kind of music? Or did he give in to commercialism, get talked into it by the record company, reaching out for what was, at the time, popular? Even if, say, he genuinely wanted to perform that kind of music, could the style of this 100 percent bebop alto sax player ever harmonize with the cool sounds of Latin American bossa nova?

Setting aside all that – after an eight-year hiatus, would Bird still be master of his instrument? Had he retained his powerful performing skills and creativity?

Truth be told, I couldn't help but feel uneasy about all that myself. I was dying to hear the music, but at the same time I felt afraid, frightened of being disappointed by what I might hear. But now, after I've listened intently to the disc over and over, I can state one thing for sure: I'd climb to the roof of a tall building and shout it so the whole town could hear. If you love jazz, or have any love for music at all, then you absolutely must listen to this charming record, the fruit of a passionate heart and a cool mind . . .

What's surprising, first of all, is the indescribable interplay between Jobim's simple, economical piano style and Bird's eloquent, uninhibited phrasing. I know you might object that Jobim's voice (he doesn't sing here so I'm referring only to his instrumental voice) and Bird's voice are totally different in quality, with contrasting, even conflicting objectives.

*We're talking about two very different voices here, so different it might
be hard to find any points they share. On top of that, neither seems to be
making much of an effort to revamp his music to fit that of the other. But
it's exactly this sense of the divergence between the two men's voices that
is the very driving force behind this uniquely lovely music.*

*I'd like you to start by listening to the first track on the A side, 'Corcovado'.
Bird doesn't play the opening theme. In fact he doesn't take up the theme
until one phrase at the end. The piece starts with Jobim quietly playing
that familiar theme alone on the piano. The rhythm section is simply mute.
The melody calls to mind a young girl seated at a window, gazing out
at the beautiful night view. Most of it is done with single notes, with the
occasional no-frills chord added, as if gently tucking a soft cushion under
the girl's shoulders.*

*And once that performance of the theme by the piano is over, Bird's
alto sax quietly enters, a faint twilight shadow slipping through a gap
in the curtain. He's there before you even realize it. These graceful,
disjointed phrases are like lovely memories, their names hidden, slipping
into your dreams. Like fine wind patterns you never want to disappear,
leaving gentle traces on the sand dunes of your heart . . .*

I'll omit the rest of the article, which is simply a further description,
with all the suitable embellishments. The above gives you an idea
of the kind of music I was talking about. Of course it's music that
doesn't actually exist. Or at least, music that *couldn't* possibly exist.

I'll wrap up that story there and talk about something that took place
years later.

For a long time I'd totally forgotten that I'd written that article back
in college. My life after school turned out to be more harried and
busy than I ever could have imagined, and that review of a make-
believe album was nothing more than a lighthearted, irresponsible
joke I'd played when I was young. But close to fifteen years later, the

article unexpectedly re-emerged into my life like a boomerang you threw whirling back at you when you least expect it.

I was in New York on business and, with time on my hands, took a walk near my hotel, ducking inside a small, secondhand-record shop I came across on East 14th Street. And in the Charlie Parker section I found, of all things, a record called *Charlie Parker Plays Bossa Nova*. It looked like a bootleg, a privately pressed recording. A white jacket with no drawing or photo on the front, just the title in sullen black letters. On the back was a list of the tracks and the musicians. Surprisingly, the list of songs and musicians was exactly as I'd invented them in college. And likewise, Hank Jones sat in for Jobim on two tracks.

I stood there, stock-still, speechless, record in hand. It felt like some small internal part of me had gone numb. I looked around again. Was this *really* New York? Yes, this was downtown New York – no doubt about it. And I was actually here, in a small used-record shop. I hadn't wandered into some fantasy world. And neither was I having a super-realistic dream.

I slipped the record out of its jacket. It had a white label, with the title and names of the songs. No sign of a record company logo. I examined the vinyl itself and found four distinct tracks on each side. I went over and asked the long-haired young guy at the register if I could take a listen to the album. No, he replied. The store turntable's broken. Sorry about that.

The price on the record was $35. I wavered for a long time about whether to buy it. In the end I left the shop empty-handed. I figured, it's got to be somebody's idea of a silly joke. Somebody, on a whim, had faked a record based on my long-ago description of an imaginary recording. Took a different record that had four tracks on each side, soaked it in water, peeled off the label and glued on a homemade one. Any way you looked at it, it was ridiculous to pay $35 for a bogus record like that.

I went to a Spanish restaurant near the hotel and had some beer and a simple dinner by myself. As I was strolling around aimlessly afterwards, a wave of regret suddenly welled up in me. I should have bought that record after all. Even if it was a fake, and way overpriced, I should have gotten it, at the very least as a souvenir of all the twists and turns my life had taken. I went straight back to East 14th Street. I hurried, but the record shop was closed by the time I got there. On the shutter was a sign that said the shop opened at 11.30 a.m. and closed at 7.30 p.m. on weekdays.

The next morning, just before noon, I went to the shop again. A middle-aged guy – thinning hair, in a disheveled, round-neck sweater – was sipping coffee and reading the sports section of the paper. The coffee seemed freshly brewed, for a pleasant smell wafted faintly through the shop. The shop had just opened, and I was the only customer. An old tune by Pharoah Sanders filtered through the small speaker on the ceiling. My guess was the man was the owner.

I thumbed through the Charlie Parker section, but the record was nowhere to be found. I was sure I'd returned it to this section yesterday. Thinking it might have got mixed in elsewhere, I rifled through every bin in the jazz section. But as hard as I looked, no luck. Had someone else bought it? I went over to the register and spoke to the middle-aged guy. 'I'm looking for a jazz record I saw here yesterday.'

'Which record?' he asked, eyes never wavering from the *New York Times*.

'*Charlie Parker Plays Bossa Nova*,' I said.

He laid down his paper, took off his thin, metal-framed reading glasses and slowly turned to face me. 'I'm sorry. Could you repeat that?'

I did. The man said nothing and took another sip of coffee. He shook his head slightly. 'There's no such record.'

'Of course,' I said.

'If you'd like *Perry Como Sings Jimi Hendrix*, we have that in stock.'

'*Perry Como Sings –*' I got that far before I realized he was pulling my leg. He was the type who kept a straight face. 'But I really *did* see it,' I insisted. 'I was sure it was produced as a joke, I mean.'

'You saw that record *here*?'

'Yesterday afternoon. Right here.' I described the record, the jacket and the songs on it. How it'd been priced at $35.

'There's gotta be some mistake. We've never had that kind of record. I do all the purchasing and pricing of jazz records myself, and if a record like that crossed my desk, I would definitely have remembered it. Whether I wanted to or not.'

He shook his head and put his reading glasses back on. He returned to the sports section, but then, as if he'd had second thoughts, he removed his glasses, smiled and gazed steadily at me. 'But if you ever do get hold of that record,' he said, 'let me listen to it, okay?'

There's one more thing that came later on. This happened long after the record-store incident (in fact, quite recently). One night I had a dream about Charlie Parker. In the dream Charlie Parker performed 'Corcovado' just for me – *for me alone*. Solo alto sax, no rhythm section.

Sunlight was shining in from some gap somewhere and Parker was standing by himself in a spot lit up by the long, vertical beam. Morning light, I assumed. Fresh, honest light, free of any superfluous meaning. Bird's face, across from me, was in deep shadow, but I could somehow make out the dark double-breasted suit, white shirt and brightly colored tie. And the alto sax he held, which was absurdly filthy, covered in dirt and rust. One bent key he'd barely kept in place by taping the handle of a spoon to it. When I saw that, I was puzzled. Even Bird wouldn't be able to get a decent sound out of that poor excuse for an instrument.

Suddenly, right then, my nose picked up an amazingly fragrant aroma of coffee. What an entrancing smell, the aroma of hot, strong black coffee. My nostrils twitched with pleasure. For all the temptations of that scent, I never took my eyes off Bird. If I did, even for a second, he might have vanished from sight.

I'm not sure why, but I knew then it was a dream. That I was seeing Bird in a dream. That happens sometimes. As I'm dreaming I know for certain *this is a dream*. And I was strangely impressed that in the midst of a dream I could catch, so very clearly, the enticing smell of coffee.

Bird finally put his lips to the mouthpiece and tentatively blew one subdued sound, as if checking the condition of the reed. And once that sound had faded away, he quietly lined up a few more notes in the same way. They floated there for a time, then gently fell to the ground, each and every one. Once they were swallowed up by the silence, Bird sent out a series of deeper, more resilient notes into the air. That's how 'Corcovado' started.

How to describe that music? Looking back on it, what Bird played for me in my dream felt less like a stream of sound than a momentary, total irradiation. I can vividly remember the music being there. But I can't reproduce it. Over time, it's faded from memory. Like being unable to describe in words the design of a mandala. What I can say is that the music reached to the deepest recesses of my soul, the very core. That kind of music existed in the world – I was certain of it – a sound that reconfigured, if ever so slightly, the very structure of your body.

'I was only thirty-four when I died,' Bird said to me. 'Thirty-four!' At least I think he was saying it to me. Since we were the only two people in the room.

I didn't know how to respond. It's hard in dreams to do the right thing. So I stayed silent, waiting for him to go on.

'Think about it – what it is to die at thirty-four,' Bird said.

I thought about how I'd feel if I'd died at thirty-four. When I'd only just begun so many things in life.

'That's right. I'd only just begun so many things myself,' Bird said. 'Only begun to live my life. But then I looked around me and it was all over.' He silently shook his head. His entire face was still in shadow, so I couldn't see his expression. His dirty, battered saxophone dangled from the strap around his neck.

'Death always comes on suddenly,' Bird said. 'But it also takes its time. Like the beautiful phrases that come into your head. It lasts an instant, yet they can linger forever. As long as it takes to go from the East Coast to the West Coast – or to infinity, even. The concept of time is lost there. In that sense, I might have been dead even while I lived out my life. But still, actual death is crushing. What's existed until then suddenly, and completely, vanishes. Returning to nothingness. In my case, that existence was *me*.'

He looked down for a time, staring at his instrument. And then spoke again.

'Do you know what I was thinking about when I died?' Bird asked. 'My mind had just one thought – a single melody. I kept on humming that melody over and over. It just wouldn't let go. That happens, right? A tune gets stuck in your head. That melody was a phrase from the third movement of Beethoven's Piano Concerto No. 1. This melody.'

Bird softly hummed the melody. I recognized it. The solo piano part.

'This is the one Beethoven melody that really swings,' Bird said. 'I've always liked his Concerto No. 1. I've listened to it I don't know how many times. The 78 rpm record with Schnabel on piano. But it's strange, don't you think? That I – Charlie Parker – died while mentally replaying, of all things, a Beethoven melody, over and over. And then came darkness. Like a curtain falling.' Bird gave a little laugh, his voice hoarse.

I had no reply. What could I possibly say about the death of Charlie Parker?

'Anyway, I need to thank you,' Bird said. 'You gave me life again, this one time. And had me play bossa nova. Nothing could make me happier. Course being alive and actually playing would have been more exciting. But even in death this was a truly wonderful experience. Since I always love new music.'

So did you appear here today in order to thank me?

'That's right,' Bird said, as if reading my mind. 'I stopped by to express my thanks. To say thank you. I hope you enjoyed my music.'

I nodded. I should have said something, but couldn't for the life of me come up with the right response.

'*Perry Como Sings Jimi Hendrix*, eh?' Bird murmured, as if recalling. And chuckled again in a hoarse voice.

And then he vanished. First his saxophone disappeared, next the light shining in from somewhere. And, finally, Bird himself was gone.

When I woke up from the dream the clock next to my bed read 3.30 a.m. It was still dark out, of course. The fragrance of coffee that should have filled the room was gone. There was no fragrance at all. I went to the kitchen and gulped down a couple of glasses of water. I sat at the dining table and tried once more to recollect, even if only in part, that amazing music that Bird had played just for me. But I couldn't recall a single note. I could, though, remember what Bird had said. Before his words faded from memory, I wrote them down as accurately as I could. When it came to the dream, that was the sole action I could take. Bird had visited my dream in order to thank me – that I recalled. To thank me for giving him the opportunity, so many years before, to play bossa nova. And he grabbed an instrument that happened to be around and played 'Corcovado' just for me.

Can you believe it?

You'd better. Because it happened.

It really did. ■

H+

Matthieu Gafsou

Introduction by Daisy Hildyard

The year before I started school I had asthma attacks so often, usually in the middle of the night, that a local charity bought a nebuliser for me. The nebuliser lived for a year in its small beige plastic case in a corner of my parents' bedroom. I remember the distinct sensation of wearing it when I had an attack, propped up in bed with sofa cushions, the latex mask moist over my skin, thick menthol-scented white fumes puffing up into my nose and mouth, and the easing feeling as my windpipe opened. My parents, I felt, were overly preoccupied with the concept of sharing, and the nebuliser had a special glamour for me because it was mine. My brother, and the other children who lived nearby, were not allowed to use it, any more than they were able to breathe through my lungs.

There is a woman wearing a respirator much like mine in one of Matthieu Gafsou's *H+* photographs, and it is a strange portrait. The proportions are traditional enough – only head and shoulders are visible – but the subject's face is largely concealed behind the mask which allows her to breathe. The woman is heavily made-up, looking through watery eyes at something beyond the camera; her lips are pursed, her hair hidden under a fluffy cream-coloured diamanté rosette beret. Ringed fingers, each nail painted a different colour, rest lightly on the tubes. The portrait is unusual because it sees the prosthesis as a part of its subject. The mask is not the incidental or even shameful apparatus of disability, but something this woman shapes and is shaped by: an integral feature of her being. Which, of course, it is.

H+ refers to transhumanism: a movement based on the idea that the human body can be improved on through scientific advancement. In the Anthropocene, nothing on Earth remains untouched by human scientific advancement: in Gafsou's *H+*, a map of augmented humanity threatens to become a transcription of everything. Gafsou's intention to map the techno-human is a vague, dreamy one, like something imagined by Jorge Luis Borges, but the resulting images are lucid and hyperreal. Seen as a collection, Gafsou's photographs gather a whole population of seemingly different technological bodies together. What links the astronaut to the pacemaker; an eighteenth-century orthotic corset to a smartphone; a lab rat to a Google mug? Gafsou gives little sense of setting or context, nobody comes or goes anywhere. Each free-floating image can only position itself in relation to the others. Not so much, then, like the kind of paper map which describes the contours of a landscape. More like a smartphone pin drop.

'Life is a window of vulnerability,' says Donna J. Haraway in *Simians, Cyborgs, and Women*. 'It seems a mistake to close it. The perfection of the fully defended, "victorious" self is a chilling fantasy.' It's unusual to catch sight of the intimate moments during which this fantasy plays out on living bodies: when the implant is inserted through a slit in the skin; the point at which the injured lab rat, suspended on hind legs with electrodes and a girdle, looks up, alert. These scenes are both tender and violent. The child's face, lit with screen-glow, or the X-rayed pacemaker in the chest, or the iodine-swabbed back in the operating theatre, are openly vulnerable. And yet in these photographs the human anatomy is merely one component of the cyborg. It has no special privileges under the camera's eye. The ubiquitous smartphone receives the same treatment as the rarest implant, which receives the same treatment as a tattooed shoulder blade or a weakening lung. The atmosphere is measured and calm. The mood is . . . there is no mood. Only the edges of blades and syringes, the healed scars and bald expanses of skin imply brutality. Many of the technological augmentations shown here have no medical necessity: they reveal nothing so much as the force of the human desire to be healed, even – especially – when there is nothing really wrong.

All this creates a strong sense of unease. No human subject in this essay can quite look Gafsou in the eye. More often than not, the machines seem more assured than the people: each object is quietly mysterious, expensive, whole. You look at a smooth-edged, brushed-titanium pacemaker, imprinted with a tiny Matisse oak leaf, and you think: I want one. In the even technocracy of *H+* there is no outdoors, no family, no dirt, no sense of humour and no such thing as natural light. It's a shadow-world: strangely familiar, all the same. The basic things – orthodontic braces, flathead screws or cups of coffee – testify to the fact that these augmentations go beyond memory: we have never known a human body without technology. Technology is both oxygen mask and gas chamber. It provides clean drinking water even as it pollutes the reservoir. Our current habits of thought are uneasy with contradiction, which is why the techno-human and the Luddite competitively mythologise themselves. The rest of us live with the contradiction, or, more accurately, we live inside it. ∎

déjeuner avec maman. J'ai dit : « Karla, c'est un déjeuner, pas une *réunion*. » Elle veut désespérément faire bonne impression. Etonnant que ça me fasse autant plaisir.

Michael est furieux contre Todd qui a recouvert une cassette VHS contenant une animation graphique pour *Oop!*, C'était une démo pour investisseurs éventuels, réalisée de sa main. Todd l'a remplacée par *Les plus belles bastons de hockey III*.

Todd et Susan ont la grippe et j'imagine qu'on est tous condamnés à l'avoir. Ethan a passé une semaine agitée. La trésorerie doit à nouveau rouler sur les jantes.

bande magnétique marron débobinée sur l'autoroute

Agrafes   **numéro de SECU**
CK-un   **panier de basket**

Si nous étions des machines, nous aurions le don d'éternité et je veux que tu comprennes ça

THE
PROSPECT
OF
IMMORTALITY

By Robert C.W. Ettinger

Frozen after clinical death--
whether you die of old age,
disease, or accident--
you may be revived & rejuvenated
by future technology,
if you make the arrangements
right now.

This is the book
that started the
cryostasis movement--
--and could extend your life
indefinitely.

New 1987 foreword by the author.

The Prospect of Immortality, by American academic and transhumanist trailblazer Robert Ettinger, is considered a bible for believers in immortality and a sort of cryogenics guidebook. He thinks 'natural man' is deficient: cryonics is the key to unlocking and making the most of his potential.

Built in Moscow in 1964, the Monument to the Conquerors of Space celebrates the achievements of Soviet space exploration. At the dawn of the twentieth century, followers of Russian cosmism believed that technology could help man achieve immortality or awaken the dead, and considered the conquest of space as the road to transcendence and the salvation of humanity. The association between transhumanism and the conquest of space occurs frequently: only an enhanced man would be capable of facing the harsh conditions of extraterrestrial colonies.

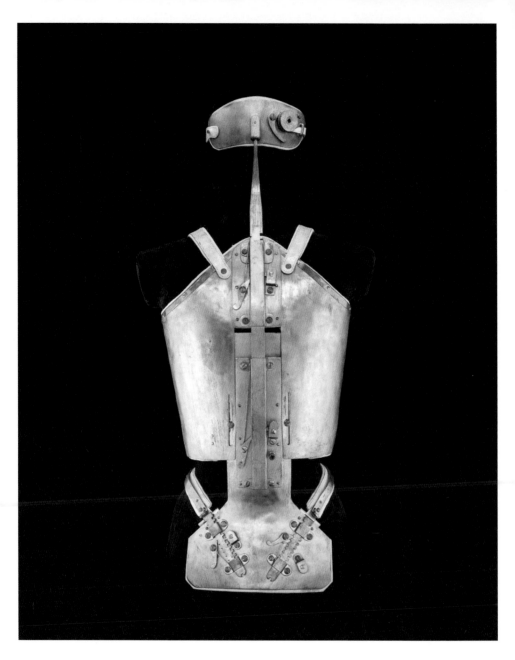

Considered one of the earliest modern prosthetists, Swiss physician Jean-André Venel (1740–1791) developed a corset for people with scoliosis, a curvature of the spine. The idea was to treat a malformation or disability. Technically, the corset is an orthotic device which compensates for an absent or deficient function, as opposed to a prosthesis, which replaces a function. Orthotics are the forerunners of the exoskeleton, the development of which is progressing quicky towards civilian and military uses.

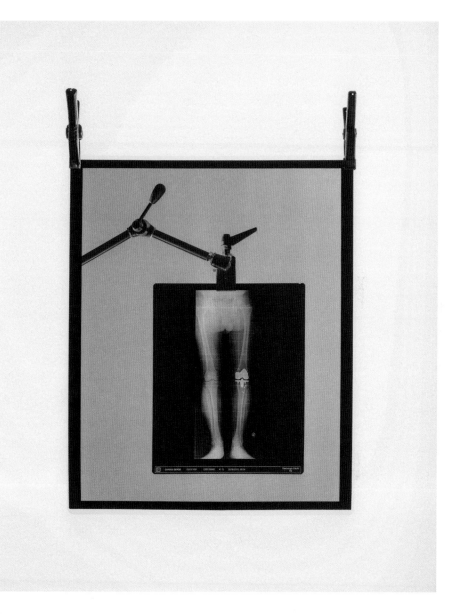

The boundary between repairing a damaged or dysfunctional body – here, my father's knee prosthesis, which is strictly therapeutic – and enhancing a healthy body may seem obvious, but it is very hard to define. When does a prosthesis leave the medical realm in the traditional sense of healing and become a means to enhance an individual? To answer that question, it is necessary to try to understand or define what health is. The World Health Organisation's (WHO) definition is clear: 'Health is a state of complete physical, mental, and social well-being and not merely the absence of disease or infirmity.' The wording, which has not changed since 1946, implies that health has a shifting, fluctuating, subjective character. This definition makes it easier to understand why many transhumanists consider their healthy bodies an incomplete vehicle that must be 'fixed' and 'fulfilled'.

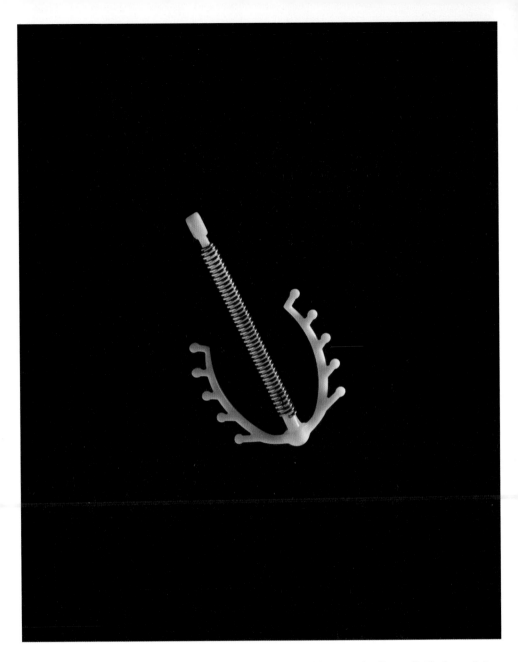

The intrauterine device (IUD) is a contraceptive invented in 1928 by Ernst Gräfenberg. It is a small object inserted into the uterus to prevent conception and, secondarily, implantation. The copper IUD releases copper ions and causes a reaction in the uterus which prevents the egg from being fertilised and/or implanted. It can remain in the uterus for several years. After removal, its effects quickly regress, increasing the chances of pregnancy. The IUD is more than a prosthesis because it changes a woman's physiology.

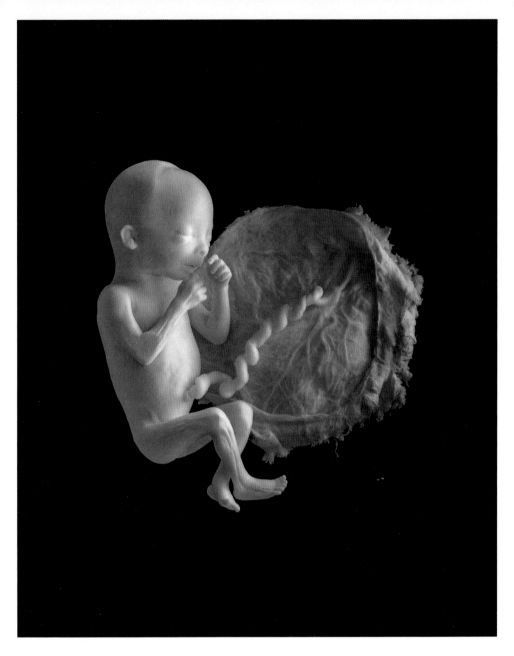

Pregnant women can have prenatal examinations to determine whether an embryo or foetus is normal. These tests lead to *in utero* therapeutic treatments or abortions, raising many ethical questions: will they eventually bring about a kind of eugenics, even though few dispute the usefulness of prenatal treatment? Transhumanists argue that these practices must be viewed as statistically improving longevity and human health.

Marie-Claude Baillif has suffered from myopathy since adolescence. Without her respirator, she would have died thirty years ago. Her website features eloquent articles about her special relationship to technology: 'My survival depends on microprocessors and electronic cards'; 'Electricity is a matter of life or death for me'; 'I love my phlegm aspirator'; 'A little battery is magical; it transforms my life'. Technological devices keep her alive.

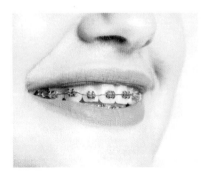

Classic orthodontic treatment using braces to align the patient's teeth. Originally therapeutic, it aimed to prevent jaw or dentition problems. Today it is also used for aesthetic purposes, establishing perfect teeth as a new norm of smile. The shift from correcting a physiological anomaly to improving appearance sees the body as a malleable, correctable object: a work in progress.

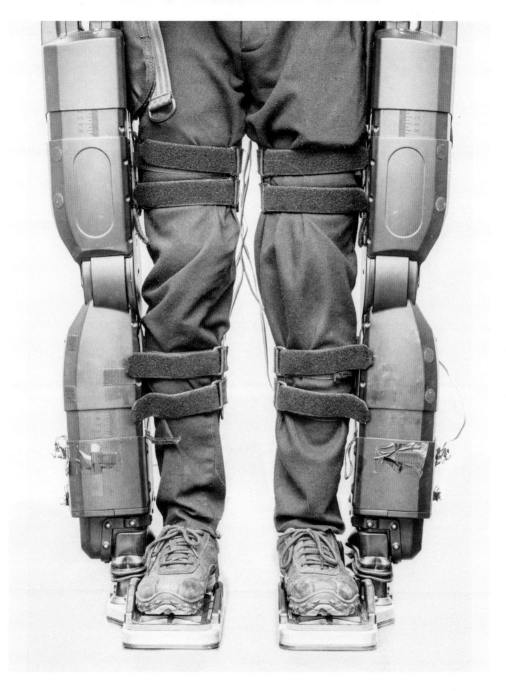

This exoskeleton can be used for therapeutic purposes or to augment the motor skills of those who wear it. Many companies sell such products as support for a strenuous activity or to treat physical handicaps. But DARPA, the Defense Advanced Research Projects Agency, is working on an exoskeleton prototype capable of turning a soldier into a nearly inexhaustible war machine.

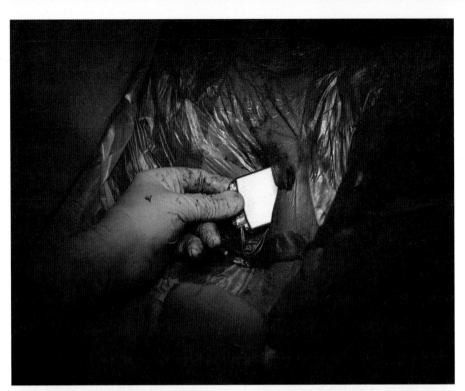

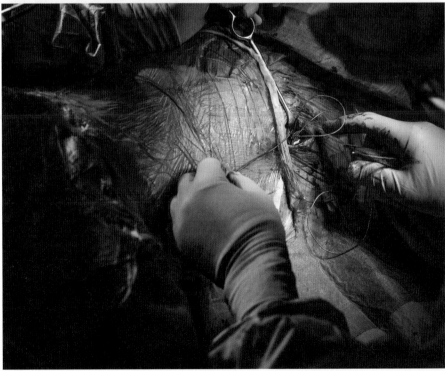

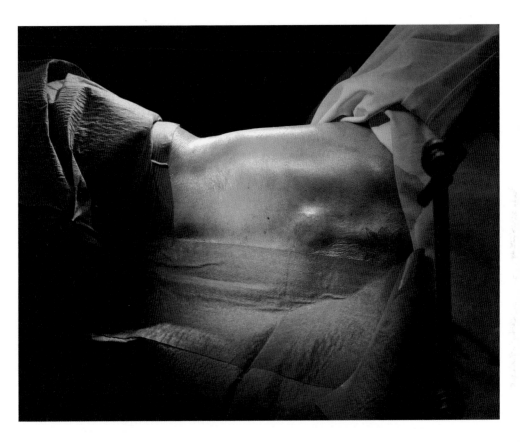

Dr Blaise Rutschmann, a chief doctor at Morges Medical Center, implanting a neurostimulator, a medical device used to treat chronic pain of neurological origin. Neurostimulation, a machine-generated electric pulse, causes paraesthesia (numbness), which alters the patient's perception of pain. It is implanted in the spinal cord during a percutaneous procedure. Then a battery is inserted in the abdomen or upper thigh and a wire (photo) connects the box to the generator. As with a pacemaker, but in a more dramatic way, the patient is wired, turning his or her body into a hybrid.

Morges Medical Center, 2 December 2016

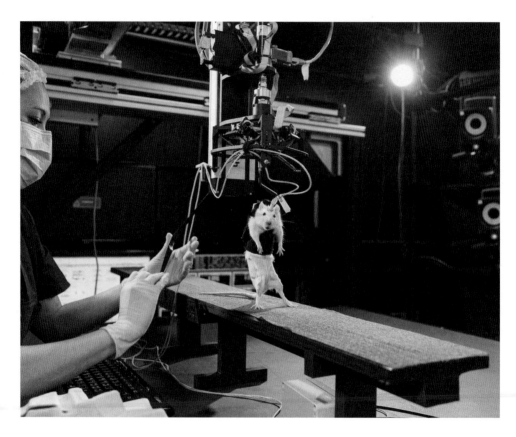

In the framework of Project reWalk, headed by Professor Grégoire Courtine of EPFL, electrodes have been implanted into this rat's injured spinal cord. The goal is for the rat to partially learn to walk again through electrical neurostimulation, accompanied by physical therapy and the use of stimulating drugs. If the spinal cord is not restored to its original condition, stimulation and physical therapy will allow a partial reconstruction of the tissues. This experiment paves the way for treating people with incapacitating spinal cord injuries.

Geneva, Campus Biotech, 22 March 2017

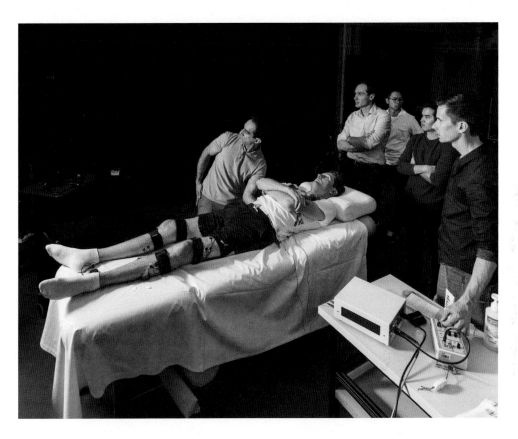

Stimulation Movement Overground (STIMO) describes epidural electrical stimulation with robot-assisted rehabilitation in patients with spinal cord injury. This is a clinical study aiming to improve the motor skills of people with injured or diseased spinal cords who have difficulties controlling their lower limbs and an extension of the reWalk experiment. The study required the participation of neuroscientists, engineers, roboticists, physicians and physical therapists. The first human patients received this type of implant in 2017.

Lausanne, CHUV (Centre Hospitalier Universitaire Vaudois), 5 April 2017

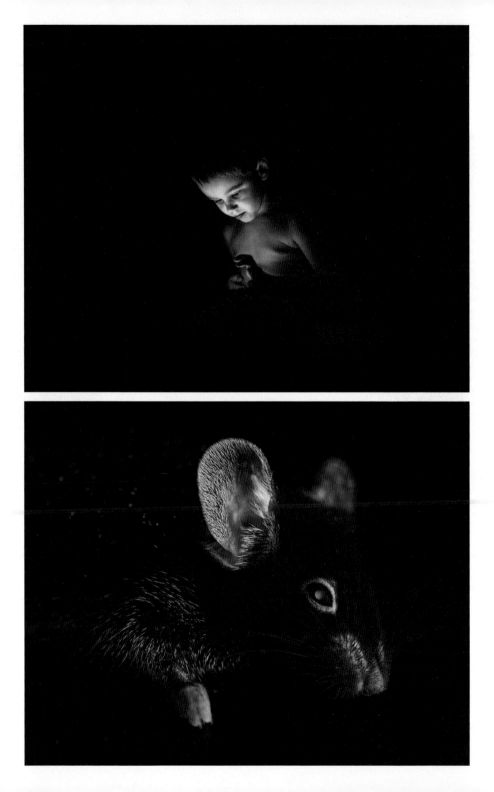

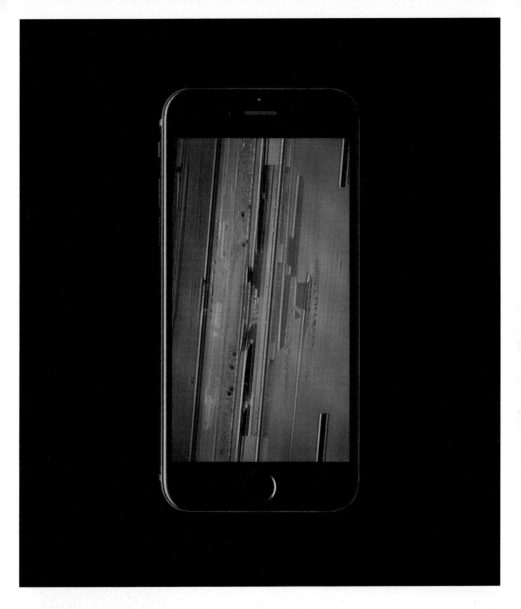

Top: In 2007, Steve Jobs launched the iPhone, which drastically increased our interaction with machines. Smartphones are now considered memory prostheses.

Bottom left: Bioluminescence in the *Aequorea victoria* jellyfish has allowed scientists to make advances using transgenesis, the transfer of genes from one species to another. Mice that have received the gene responsible for bioluminescence in the *Aequorea victoria* glow when exposed to UV rays. Researchers use this property as a marker allowing them to analyse the growth of tissues, organs, tumours, etc.

Freiburg, 30 March 2017

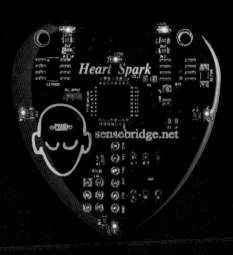

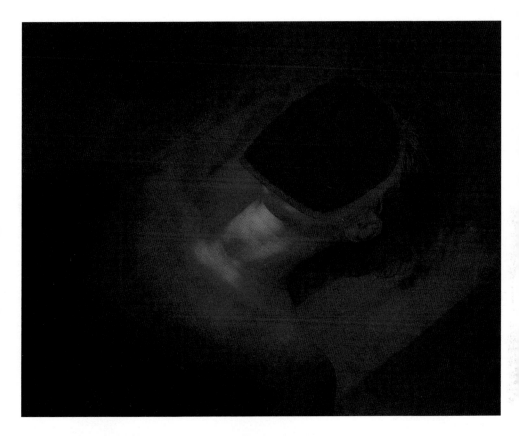

Top: If worn every day for five minutes, this anti-ageing, light-therapy mask supposedly makes whoever wears it look younger. The sales pitch borrows from medical discourse, even though it is a beauty product, much like anti-ageing cream. The device is part of the already dominant ideology of the perfect body while adding the cult of technology as a way to save it from decrepitude. It is a geeky, cheap, non-invasive version of plastic surgery.

Left: Some people wear necklaces that blink to the rhythm of their heartbeat. Others have had devices implanted allowing them to 'feel' the magnetic north. In either case, these are demonstrative gadgets that prefigure objects with more potential. External appendages, they are outward signs of participating in a project: their function is therefore quite superficial. They are symbols, futuristic substitutes for crosses or religious medals.

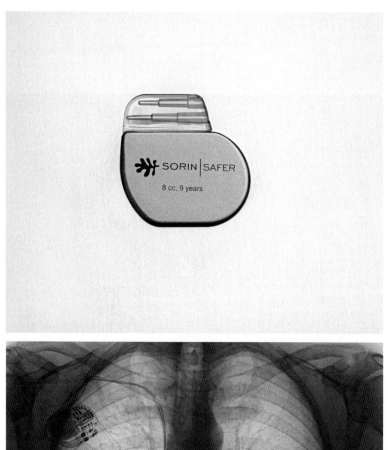

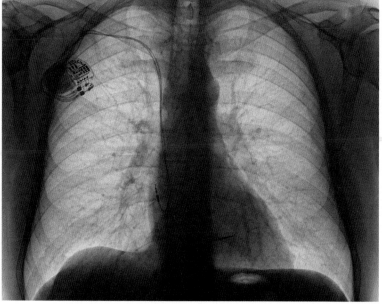

Top: The pacemaker is a device implanted in the body that sends electric pulses to stimulate the heart muscle to regulate the heartbeat. It is made up of a battery (photo) and electrodes connected to the patient's heart. Some are also automatic defibrillators. The same type of device can also be used to relieve certain kinds of chronic pain: the electric pulses act directly on the spinal cord. One of the first implanted electric devices, it is in that sense emblematic of the mechanisation of the human body.

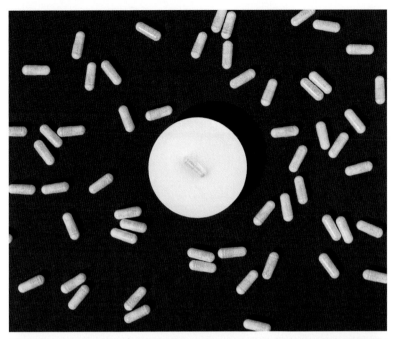

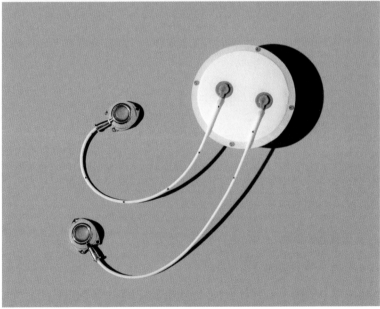

Bottom: MailPan is an implant filled with stem cells that can secrete insulin for diabetics. The technological challenge is twofold: manufacturing a membrane capable of releasing oxygen and insulin while remaining impervious to the immune system when it attacks the stem cells; and finding cells that will manufacture insulin in an optimal way. When a syringe is inserted every three to six months, two ports placed under the skin allow the stem cells that have become inactive to be removed and replaced by new ones.

Top: Born in 1918, centenarian Jeanne-Marie Dudan enjoys drinking strong espresso, the only nootropic substance, along with tea, she has ever consumed. 'There are those who recommend, sometimes with ridiculous exaggeration, this liqueur's beneficial properties, while others consider any amount harmful. To the latter we can quote Fontenelle's reply to a doctor who told him that coffee is a slow-acting poison. "It is slow," he said. "I've been drinking it every day for the past 80 years." That, I believe, is called irrefutable proof.' From Dr Hippolyte-Alexandre Trifet, *Histoire et physiologie du café. De son action sur l'homme, à l'état de santé et à l'état de maladie*, 1846.

Left: These 'total' foods are not dietary supplements but food substitutes. They are symptomatic of abandoning the body as a locus of pleasure and how much it is increasingly considered a vehicle, the functioning of which must be preserved. During my discussions, especially with the Russian transhumanist Danila Medvedev, I heard that, 'thanks to this type of diet, we are gradually moving away from solid food while saving time and protecting our health'. When I asked him about physical pleasure, he replied that on the scale of eternity – his horizon – that type of pleasure becomes trivial. The sales arguments put forward by companies that sell this powder are nutritional perfection, the quality of the products, respect for animals (veganism), and the saving of time.

The quantified-self movement advocates measuring physiological data in order to be healthier. It is part of the trend towards predictive medicine and increasing life expectancy. The quantified self uses tools connected to applications. They are usually external, but many companies are working on integrating them into the body. For example, heart rate, activity during sleep, the blood oxygen rate, or physical activity can be measured. Quantified self allows individuals to create their own connected space and, in a way, become an information system.

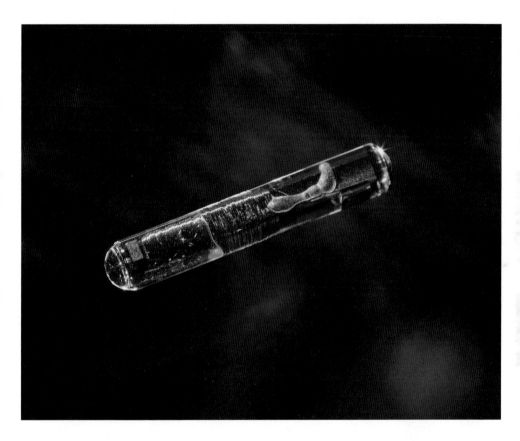

The size of a grain of rice, the NFC/RFID (Near Field Communication/Radio Frequency Identification) microchip can be implanted under the skin. In general, tattoo artists perform the operation. NFC/RFID is a way to store and retrieve remote data. The latest implantable microchips combine both technologies, leaving their uses up to their hosts. They can store medical data, passwords and small bits of information, or interface with other electronic devices, such as smartphones. Highly regarded by biohackers, they symbolise the transformation of humans into cyborgs.

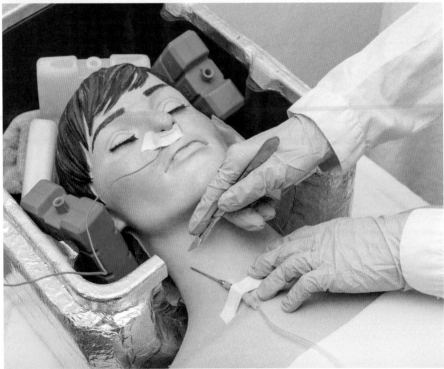

Top: KrioRus's brand-new Russian facility. The vats contain cryogenised brains and whole bodies awaiting the day when science can wake them up.

Top left: Igor Trapeznikov, Alexey Samykin, Valerija Pride, Danila Medvedev, Sergey Evfratov and Ivan Stepin are members of Russia's transhumanist movement. In the absence of any restrictive legal framework, they founded KrioRus, one of the world's three cryonics companies. They believe in immortality.

Bottom left: KrioRus not only deep-freezes corpses but also trains cryogenisation devotees in how to prepare them. The bodily fluids are drained; otherwise deep-freezing will break the cell tissue, making a future reawakening less likely. The depot, in the countryside outside Moscow, is the hub of their activities.

Hannes Sjöblad, activist and co-founder of the Swedish biohacking organisation BioNyfiken, is a leading promoter of transhumanism in Europe. In Paris in 2015, he held the first Implant Party, where candidates received their microchip implants in public. He earns his living by giving companies strategic advice about technology and lecturing on the 'enhanced human'.

Paris, *Futur en Seine*, 30 June 2017

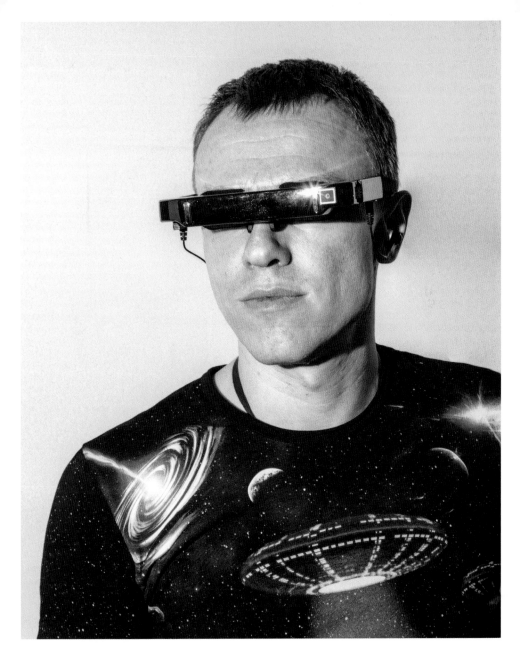

Igor Trapeznikov, a member of Russia's transhumanist movement, wears several handmade experimental implants, including a device that turns sights into sounds, which could prove useful for blind or vision-impaired people. He also has various handmade microchip implants, replacing his credit card and house keys, for example.

Moscow, 21 June 2017

Neil Harbisson considers himself a cyborg. Afflicted with achromatopsia, a rare form of colour blindness, he has had a prosthesis called Eyeborg implanted into his skull that converts colours into sound waves. Harbisson advocates creative enhancement of the human and sometimes distances himself from transhumanism, which he thinks is stuck in stereotyped or commercial depictions. His view is more that of an artist than a disciple of technoscience. He takes pride in being the first human to appear with a visible prosthesis in a passport photo.

Munich, 15 July 2015

In 2013, Google launched Calico (California Life Company) at the secret Google X Lab complex. The company's goal is to combat ageing and its related maladies and eventually kill death. So far, Calico has not marketed any products.

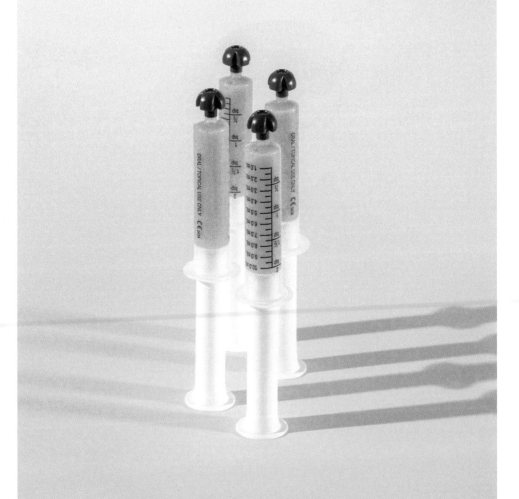

Top: A host of home laboratory kits are available for purchase online. They can include everything a DIY biologist needs, from instruments to plasmids and the substances to cultivate them in Petri dishes, from genetically modified cells and bacteria to bioluminescent cuttlefish or fireflies.

Left: Transhumanists often say that even apparently healthy bodies are sick and imperfect and that technology, like chemical prosthetics or dietary supplements, are a means to achieve physical perfection. 'Nootropics (from *noos*, "mind", and *tropos*, "bend"), also known as smart drugs and cognitive enhancers, are drugs, supplements, and other substances that improve cognitive function, particularly executive functions, memory, creativity, or motivation, in healthy individuals. Generally recognized as safe at low doses, nootropics are promoted in transhumanism as a means to improve living conditions or achieve specific goals, such as increasing motivation.' From Wikipedia: 'Nootropics' article.

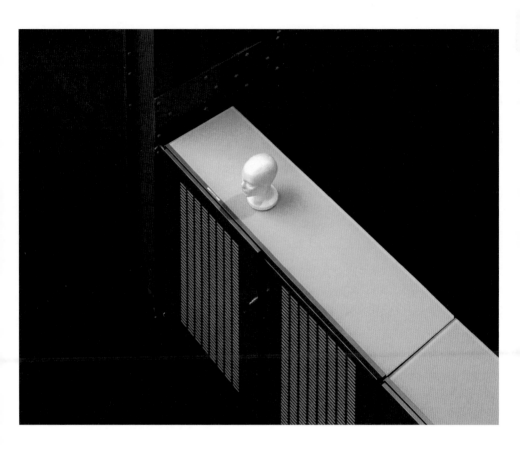

19.
internationales
literaturfestival
berlin
11 – 21 09 2019

ELIZABETH ACEVEDO USA
ANDRÉ ACIMAN EGYPT/USA
CHIMAMANDA NGOZI ADICHIE NIGERIA/ USA
JOSÉ EDUARDO AGUALUSA ANGOLA
NOURI AL-JARRAH SYRIA/ UK
BENYAMIN INDIA
MAXIM BILLER GERMANY
HUSSEIN BIN HAMZA SYRIA/ GERMANY
ESI EDUGYAN CANADA
WOLFRAM EILENBERGER GERMANY
DIDIER ERIBON FRANCE
PETINA GAPPAH ZIMBABWE
ROBERT HABECK GERMANY
FLORIAN ILLIES GERMANY
ERIN ENTRADA KELLY USA
MUSTAFA KHALIFA SYRIA/ FRANCE
ROBERT MACFARLANE UK
NICOLAS MATHIEU FRANCE
EILEEN MYLES USA
TOMMY ORANGE USA
SERGIO RAMÍREZ NICARAGUA/ SPAIN
RODRIGO REY ROSA GUATEMALA
MÅRTEN SANDÉN SWEDEN
RAOUL SCHROTT AUSTRIA
DAG SOLSTAD NORWAY
OCEAN VUONG VIETNAM/ USA
XUN LIU CHINA

full programme:
literaturfestival.com

FIELD NOTES
ON A MARRIAGE

Te-Ping Chen

It was not a place, Gao said, that he wanted to go. 'It's not a very nice country,' he said. 'Dirty, but without being charming.' We had only two weeks and we should spend it someplace romantic, a real honeymoon destination, he said. I protested. As a child my favorite doll was a Chinese porcelain girl with stiff black plaits and gold-veined red pajamas, and tiny satin booties that matched. I'd always wanted to go. 'I'd like to see where you're from,' I told him, but he shook his head: another time.

We had met that previous October. I must have seen him on campus before, though I don't know that I would have noticed him. If I had, I would have thought he was a graduate student. He had that look, somewhat underfed, and habitually wore a leather coat that in later years I would tease him about, zipped tightly around his middle. It made him look like an aspiring motorcycle rider instead of what he was, a newly minted associate professor of German with a few promising publications under his belt.

The coffee shop where I usually worked was crowded that day. He arrived and looked inquiringly at the seat beside me, and I smiled and pushed aside the anthropology syllabus I was working on. I noted the book he was reading, a Pushkin biography, and we got to talking. Gao had a funny demeanor that took a while to parse: restrained, almost haughty at first, but sometimes he'd break out in a hearty bout of laughter that took you by surprise. It took me. He was very entertained, for example, by the fact that I'd grown up on a farm.

'A farm!' he said, and burst out laughing. 'No, really. Goats, cows, that kind of thing?'

'Alfalfa, actually,' I said, smiling. 'Indiana.' I couldn't tell what he found so amusing, but he was so pleased I found myself laughing as well.

As I later learned, the stop-off for coffee was part of his post-gym routine, prior to heading back to his office. He was, in all things, rigidly disciplined. He spent two hours a day at the gym working through a precise program he'd designed himself, quadriceps and laterals, a routine that sounded to me like a series of math problems. Then he'd head home and eat a half-pound of Brussels sprouts, boiled in a bag on the stove. He never touched anything with sugar, nothing fried. 'I'm not interested in food,' he told me.

At first it was a walk in a botanical garden, lunch at a brightly lit cafe, a visit to a weekend flea market. I had almost reconciled myself to thinking we were simply friends when, during a student chamber-music concert one evening, Gao slipped his hand over mine. Afterwards, standing on the sidewalk, we exchanged some chaste, dry-lipped kisses, hands fumbling experimentally about each other as though we were teenagers.

He didn't like to talk about himself, something that I found refreshing, almost old-fashioned after so many years spent in a confessional university environment. 'You're from China,' I said on our second meeting as we strolled amid the spiked leaves of the botanical garden, a section devoted to North American desert plants. I looked at him expectantly, and he nodded, as though this was part of a series of formalities he had to endure. 'Which part?'

'Someplace you've never heard of,' he said, and named it. 'It's a backwater,' he said.

'Rickshaws and rice paddies?' I grinned, and he shrugged. 'You could say that.' I asked him how he'd learned German, but there, too, he was laconic, saying only that he'd gotten a high-school scholarship to go to Europe, and that he'd stayed. 'I haven't been back since I was sixteen,' he said indifferently, meaning home, in a tone that discouraged questions.

He wanted to know all about me, though, to hear about my fieldwork, my family, he had a greediness for knowledge of me I'd never experienced before, at once intoxicating and intensely flattering. He wanted to know everything from childhood nicknames to details of my school science fairs, studying me as intently as if he might have to someday defend our relationship to a panel of colleagues.

'You're so self-sufficient,' Gao said to me, early in our courtship. It was after he'd visited my apartment for the first time and opened the refrigerator to see the rows of Tupperware neatly stacked, the zshopping list registered in a precise hand. He'd meant it as a compliment, and after a pause, I thanked him.

One Saturday six weeks later we spent the afternoon in my bedroom, naked in the bright sunlight, inspecting each other curiously, without desire, as though we were museum curators cataloguing idiosyncrasies: the raised mole here, a pale depression of stretch marks there. The afternoon light came in through the window, irradiating every body hair. I felt lazy, warm and speculative. We'd been half-watching a Spanish soap opera, me periodically offering up translations; the plot (involving a priest officiating a wedding who halfway through the ceremony took off a false beard and revealed himself to be the bride's lover) kept us laughing.

'You've never done it, right?' he said, when we turned the TV off. 'Gotten married.'

'No,' I said, staring at the ceiling. It hadn't bothered me. There were a lot of things I hadn't done: run a marathon, become a doctor, developed a taste for Mediterranean food. There were a lot of things I had.

'Why don't we?' Gao said.

'You're joking,' I said.

'Why not?' he said. I turned over then, and looked at him. He was lying with his head propped on one arm, gazing at me with an unreadable expression.

'We hardly know each other.'

'I'm serious. We get along, don't we?'

I flopped back onto the bed, astonished. 'Okay,' I said, still watching him to see if he was kidding. 'Let's do it.'

He rolled over on top of me and tickled the underside of my chin with his finger. 'You're sure, *häschen*?' he said. It meant bunny, an animal I never liked – too anxious, too red-eyed – but I didn't mind the endearment when he used it.

I nodded. 'Okay,' he said, and rose, humming. 'What are you doing tomorrow, then?' I reached out, laughing, trying to pull him back down, but he went to the kitchen, where I heard the tap being turned on and the sound of ice being cracked and water running. Even after living in the US for more than a decade, Gao still couldn't get over the fact that he could drink from the tap, could drink a dozen glasses a day.

After our marriage, Gao's relentless questions about me stopped, as though I were a topic that his restless brain had sufficiently mastered. We folded ourselves into each other's lives neatly, seamlessly. He moved into my apartment with just two suitcases' worth of clothes; all his books and papers lived at his office. Our dish rack held two plates and two mugs, mine maroon and his green, that we rinsed and replaced every night.

That summer, we went to Indiana to see my parents, who had clamored to meet him for months. For a week, Gao shucked corn from the market with my mom and rode a tractor on the farm with my dad. At nights we sat with the porch door open and listened to the crickets in the grass. Usually I grew antsy there, felt stranded, but I could see something about the life appealed to Gao. He was the ideal guest, eating things he wouldn't usually touch – bacon, thick pancakes – and asked my parents endless questions about the farm in a way that reminded me of how he'd been when we'd first met. They responded as I had: flattered, instantly wooed. (They also asked me if he was a Chinese spy: 'He's so fit!' my mother said, and looked almost disappointed when I said no.)

'Actually, Gao grew up on a farm, too,' I told them over breakfast on our second day.

'No kidding!' my dad said.

I saw Gao hesitate. 'Not really,' he said.

'I thought you said you grew up in the countryside?'

'More like a small town,' he said. 'My mom was a high-school principal,' he added. 'My dad was a government official.'

I hadn't known either of these things, and it made me feel foolish, exposed. I got up, annoyed, and went out to the porch with a glass in hand, expecting him to follow, but he didn't, and after a few minutes I returned, not wanting to make a scene.

In the months that followed, Gao was often away, working late at his office or at the gym. I didn't mind, I still hadn't accustomed myself to spending so much time with another person. Though we took many of our weekday meals apart, we ate dinner together at a Sichuanese restaurant every Friday, dining on petal-soft pieces of white fish cooked with blood-red chilies that made my lips tingle.

Now and then we'd go for a hike along the fire trails up in the hills. We were good companions. Only occasionally did it occur to me to wish for something more. For our first anniversary – paper – he'd given me a beautifully fashioned set of origami boxes that he'd made himself. I'd opened them, expecting a gift inside, and flushed when I found them empty, realizing my mistake, hoping he hadn't noticed.

At night these memories still swim up to me, unbidden. Most of the time I pat them on the head and send them away, releasing them back into dark waters. I tell myself it doesn't do to fixate too much on the dead: apart from everything else, they can't answer you.

The flight to China was a distance of 6,000 miles and seventeen hours. Flight attendants came through the aisles offering tea and almond cookies. I leaned my forehead against the chilly, black window and watched a miniature plane trace a dotted line across the blue and green map on the seatback screen. As we neared our destination, the airline played a welcome video of misty pagodas and lily pads spread over a pond flecked with golden fish, observed by a woman in trailing magenta robes who carried a paper parasol.

The scene outside the airport nearest Gao's hometown was considerably less appealing: a sprawling monochrome of warehouses that ran untidily for miles, hardly the small town Gao had described, though I supposed it might still have been one when he left. As we entered its outskirts, I felt the cab driver eyeing me, a woman alone in his backseat. 'America,' he said. It wasn't a question. 'Yes,' I said, in an attitude of brightness, but he just nodded.

After an hour, we reached the hotel, a concrete block streaked with brown rust stains that said Gold Phoenix Villa. Tinny advertisements blared from a shop selling hosiery across the street. Inside, the hotel's lobby was cold and hung with a faded watch ad featuring a Western couple. The woman had sallow cheeks and a wide nose that wouldn't have made the cut in an American advertisement, posing beside a blond man who smiled with the grimace of a serial killer appearing in a family portrait.

Gao's mother met me there the next morning. She wore her hair in tightly wound curls and a dark green skirt with flounces, and came straight over and linked her arm through mine with a warmth that surprised me. Neither she nor Gao's father came to his funeral, and I had tried not to judge them for it, unsuccessfully.

'You're here,' she said, and briskly steered me outside, not quite making eye contact. 'Welcome.'

'I'm so pleased to meet you,' I said, flushing. 'I've wanted to come here for so long.'

Outside in the parking lot, she slid her legs behind the wheel of a dark grey sedan and made an elaborate performance of adjusting the mirrors. 'New,' she said. 'My baby,' she said, and laughed, as though to make sure I knew it was a joke.

We drove for a while, passing crude shops with pasteboard signs, mostly identical in style but on some of them you could tell what was being sold by their emblems: a sheep standing in front of a pot (presumably a restaurant of some sort), a series of pipe fittings. All around us, rain darkened the road.

She had not invited me to visit, I had invited myself, and as we drove without speaking, I felt a growing awareness of the fact. 'It's good to be here,' I said at last. 'Gao told me so much about this place.'

It wasn't true, and perhaps she sensed it, simply nodding. There was a temple, she said, she'd take me. There was a museum, as well, not very large. What else did I want to see?

'Anything from Gao's childhood,' I said.

She said there wasn't much left: the government had torn down their old family home years ago and replaced it with a shopping mall. The school had been converted into government offices.

I was disappointed, but tried not to show it. 'I'd still like to see it,' I said.

'The mall?' The fact that Gao's mother had been a high-school principal showed, I thought: beyond the perm and flouncy skirt, she had an aura of steely competence to her.

I said yes, but she shook her head impatiently. 'There's nothing there. You should see some history. This city has 4,000 years of history.'

When I agreed, she nodded and turned on the radio, drowning out the need for further conversation.

Gao hadn't been a popular child, but he'd commanded a certain amount of respect because of his mother's position. Other parents, in particular, fawned on him. They passed him sweets when picking up their children after school, they praised his cleverness. Eventually he drew to him a small coterie of boys like himself, bright and a little insecure. Their names regularly topped the list of students with the best grades, weekly posted outside the school gates for all the parents to see.

But there was one boy who always topped the list for both reading and math, not of their group, whom they called Mouse. He was one of the boarders, he'd come from a village a day's travel away. Gao shrugged when I'd asked about the nickname. 'He was small,' he said.

As the high-school entrance exam neared, students studied six days a week, eleven hours a day, and Gao hardest of all, because everyone expected him to do well. 'You can't imagine what the pressure was like,' he told me. 'It was cruel.'

At the time, we were in Germany on our honeymoon and he'd taken me to see the university where he'd done his degree. We'd visited the carrel in the library where he used to study and the classroom where he'd defended his dissertation, and it was there that he'd paused, and for a while it didn't seem like he'd ever want to move again. 'So you can imagine how glad I was to get away,' he said.

At the temple, I asked Gao's mother what her son was like as a child. 'He was a good student,' she said. We were standing side by side, staring at a statue of a robed god painted blue with vermillion eyes. She had linked her arm through mine, making it hard to see her expression, though when I asked her what else she could remember, I could feel her sigh at my side, just a little.

'He was very well-behaved. Hard-working, good at his studies.'

Something about her repetition of these qualities annoyed me, and I walked away on the pretext of examining a placard more closely. 'Was he a happy kid?' I asked.

'Yes, of course,' she said, a sudden defensiveness in her voice.

'It's a shame he never came back here,' I said.

'Not really. Why should he?' she said.

We resumed walking. The temple was composed of a series of courtyards, with one long corridor dotted with small niches containing scores of Buddhas cast in shiny gold plastic. The green and white and maroon that swirled in fanciful shapes about the ceiling's wooden beams looked newly painted, and there were heaps of new tiles and nails scattered carelessly about. A sign said that the temple was destroyed in a fifteenth-century fire and rebuilt, and damaged in an earthquake and rebuilt again.

'It has a history of six hundred years,' Gao's mother said. 'Very old. Not like your America.'

Further on, she urged me to stand in front of a Buddha statue, and snapped a photo of me with my camera. Already that afternoon she had had me pose before an inscribed stele, a rock formation and a small pavilion. My cheeks hurt from smiling.

'How about over there?' she asked, gesturing to another courtyard. I went, not wanting to disappoint her. She took another photo, one I didn't smile for. At last, to my relief, we began moving toward the exit.

'Would Gao ever have come here?' I asked.

She thought about it, then shook her head. 'It's mostly for tourists.'

'Well,' I said, and didn't have anything else to add. 'It's very pretty,' I said finally.

After two years of our marriage, Gao seemed to draw still further into himself. He spent increasingly long hours at the office, but his publications were sparse and failed to gain attention; he'd recently been passed over for a grant that before he would have won easily. The German department wasn't large and had just hired a young Ukrainian scholar fresh from his PhD whom everyone was looking to as its next star. Once I'd come into Gao's office and found him with his head in his arms. I'd stood there for a few minutes, watching him, before touching him on the shoulder. He said he'd been sleeping.

We were celebrating our second anniversary when Gao told me the rest of Mouse's story. We'd gone to the Sichuanese restaurant downtown, where the maître d' had given us a table beside the big plate-glass window. The waiter brought us fish, rice and cubes of tofu cooked with chilies, bristling with dashes of green onion. A cluster of unopened chrysanthemums sat between us, curled like tiny fists in a small vase. It had been a long day for Gao at the office, a department meeting and hours spent revising a paper that had already been rejected twice for publication, and he was quiet. The restaurant was quiet, too – it was a weeknight – and I wondered if the waiters could tell there was something wrong. Outside, it had grown dark, and I imagined that we looked like a pair of silent actors to passersby outside, seen through the lit window as though onstage.

'Tell me something,' I said to him, when the silence had gone on too long.

'Like what?'

'Anything. Something I don't know about you.'

'You first,' he said. With a fork, he began to debone the fish, extracting each wispy bone with his fingertips.

'Okay,' I said. 'Are you sure you don't want to order some wine?' He nodded and placed his hand over mine. It was a gesture I noticed he was using more and more; lately it had stopped feeling confiding and more like someone gently closing your mouth.

Finally, I told him the story of our first cat. It was supposed to be mine, but it never liked me much, always preferred my parents' bed. I used to sneak into my parents' room to snatch it and make it sleep with me, I told him, only to wake to hear it scratching at the door, trying to get out. 'She died when I was in college,' I told him, attempting a laugh. 'Up until the end, she didn't like me very much.'

He smiled absently and wiped his mouth. 'Stupid cat.'

'Your turn,' I said, and waited. He folded his napkin and put it on the table. 'I'll tell you something,' he said, slowly, 'since you ask.'

He told me that when he and his friends turned fourteen, somehow it was decided among them that Mouse was a Japanese spy. He'd come from far away, no one knew his antecedents. He looked strange, with hair that was paler than the rest. ('I know now it was probably malnutrition,' Gao said.) He was unbeatable in tests, 'almost militaristic', they told each other. He had a funny white shirt they grew convinced was cut in a Japanese style.

For months, they watched him closely for clues. Someone had seen him make a nighttime trip to the bathroom, it was possible he was meeting secret accomplices. A teacher had kept him after class, perhaps the two were in league. At some point he went back to his village for a month, it was said his grandmother had died, but Gao and his friends knew better, Mouse was training in the hills. When he came back, it was as though all their fears were confirmed. The attack he was training for would come any day now, they said.

Gradually their plot took shape. 'It was a game at first,' Gao said. He stole some rat poison from the janitor. 'We joked it was rat poison for a mouse,' he said. Another boy, not to be outdone, befriended Mouse, started eating lunches with him. A third took still more rat poison in case the first attempt failed. It was the second boy who slipped a generous dose of it into Mouse's stir-fried eggplant at the canteen.

'Oh God,' I said. 'What happened?'

Gao looked at me as though I'd asked a foolish question. 'He died, of course,' he said tiredly.

I didn't know what to say. 'Did they ever catch anyone?'

He didn't answer me for a while. 'One boy,' he said eventually. 'The boy who gave him the poison.'

When the boy's parents came from their home village in the mountains to take the body away, the mother hysterical, the man wooden and stunned, they realized their mistake: Mouse's parents were poor villagers, speaking in a tongue so heavy and coarse the school administrators had trouble understanding them.

'And then you went to Germany,' I said. He agreed with me. 'And then I went to Germany.'

That spring when the rains came, ants invaded our apartment, criss-crossing the kitchen in wobbly black lines. We bought a tub of petroleum and erected walls of it across the linoleum to try and stop their steady march. When that failed, Gao stood guard with the hose of a vacuum cleaner at the ready, determined to catch any escapees. The morning glory vines that clung to our front porch unfurled themselves in purple trumpets. We started talking about having a family. We were going to begin trying any day now, we said.

Then came a night when I'd fallen asleep early over a stack of student papers and awoke just after dawn. Gao had said he'd be back after a late-night bout of grading at his office, but his side of the bed was undisturbed, the apartment empty. I made myself some coffee, called his office, paced for a while impatiently, and finally went to the car.

The morning chill was still in the air, the kind of cold that makes you expect birdsong. Gao's building was locked. I rapped on the door, but there was no reply. I found the facilities management office and waited until it opened. A janitor accompanied me back and unlocked the door: Gao's chair was pushed tidily in, the place empty. I flicked on the light anyway, futilely. 'Thanks,' I said, smiling, trying not to seem alarmed. 'He must have lost track of time somewhere – I'll check the library.'

He wasn't there. I tried the gym, searching through rows of undergraduates with their ellipticals, neat ponytails and elastic skin, but Gao wasn't among them. I stopped at the cafe where we'd first met; the owner was just unlocking the doors, bleary-eyed. Finally I circled back to our home, maybe he'd returned in my absence.

He hadn't. I made myself more coffee and sat on the couch. I put a blanket on. I thought perhaps he was angry with me. I scoured my mind to try and remember any unintended slight. I sat there all day, reheating bowls of soup, and when the phone rang at 4 p.m., it was a moment before I could bring myself to answer. It was the local police, called in by the parks department. They'd found him.

It was an elderly man out walking his Border collie in the hills who'd made the report. Gao's body was dangling from a tree, face black, still clad in his leather jacket, ID and car keys in his breast pocket. He'd been there all night. His car had been found in the otherwise empty parking lot, an index card with my name and number written in his hand on the dashboard. I searched the apartment for days, but there wasn't anything else, no apology, no note of explanation. He had been private in almost everything throughout our marriage, and he was private, too, in his death.

The days proceeded in his absence: phone calls with friends and funeral homes, details that needed arranging. Friends waited for confidences, but I had none to share. Our marriage had been brief, I said, I was sorry it was over. His life had been his own, I told myself, to do with it what he would, and he did.

After the funeral, though, that sentiment cracked, and a chasm opened up within me. At night I buried myself under a pile of his shirts as I lay in bed, imagining the child we might have had together (his cheeks, my eyes). I found myself crying in grocery aisles and at the lecture podium, tears that came on quickly and tapered with equal speed. I resigned myself to their appearances; it was like a new cardiac rhythm or myopia, something unfamiliar but irrevocably now a part of me.

I kept his mug and plate in the dish rack. I kept a pair of his loafers by the front door. I began to feel an unreasonable resentment toward those whose marriages had been ruptured by affairs or neglect or abandonment, for their clarity of answers, or the fact that they could pick up the phone, at least, and demand them.

Whole weeks would go by and I couldn't remember what had happened in them.

Fall passed, and then winter. When I looked up from my desk it was spring, and the dean was standing in the doorway. A leave of absence might be a good idea, she said. I had missed three of my classes in the past month, and students were complaining.

Not long after that, I found myself in the travel section of a bookshop and suddenly – despite Gao's insistence on its remoteness – there it was, listed in a China guide: a brief entry on his hometown. It didn't sound very enticing, it was described as a *dingy stopover with good connection links and some adequate hotels*, with two temples listed and one museum. But still it sent a jolt through me, to see it printed in black and white, a real place, with clearly listed directions on how to get there. A month later, when classes finished for the summer, I was on a plane.

After the museum – a crowded affair of jostling children competing to peer into plexiglass boxes containing oxidized bronze and old coins – Gao's mother drove us silently back to their apartment on the town's outskirts, past the recently poured roads and freshly built high-rises dotting the landscape. Now and then we passed a few soon-to-be-demolished low-rises that still showed signs of inhabitants: a line of laundry here, a toy tricycle there, a stooped man wandering with his hands behind his back.

Their apartment was a cramped two-bedroom on the eleventh floor, and as we entered, Gao's father shuffled to greet us in rubber slippers. He looked older than his wife and wore a soft-brimmed flat black cap, and chuckled in greeting on seeing me. I liked him straightaway. 'Hello,' he said. He offered me some tiny candies wrapped in foil, chuckling some more, it appeared to be a tic of his. '*Ni hao*,' I quavered, and he beamed again.

'Please sit,' Gao's mother said, and arranged me on the couch before heading to the kitchen. My legs ached, and I didn't protest. At the museum she had hovered by my side, reading the mangled English descriptions aloud to me as though I were a child, and if I missed a single display case, she would gesture me over to study its contents.

Gao's father sank into a chair beside me, looking pleased. The place had a transient feel, nothing on the walls. I tried to speak with him, but he didn't understand me, and together instead we turned our attentions to the television, where an androgynous-looking host was interviewing a rail-thin woman who clutched a curly-haired dog to her chest.

'Are you sure I can't help?' I called to Gao's mother, craning my neck around the corner.

She stuck her head out from the doorway. 'No need,' she said. In one hand, she waved a slick-shelled, gray shrimp at me, antennae twitching in a way that briefly made it look alive. 'It's very easy.'

From the kitchen, I could hear the pot sizzle, and when the androgynous interviewer's segment was over I got up and followed the smell. Gao's mother was standing before a cutting board, mincing garlic into a sticky crumb, ginger into matchsticks. 'That smells good,' I said.

'There are some pictures in the other room,' she said, without turning around. 'You can have a look.'

The study was strewn with books and papers in a way that struck me as at odds with the clipped decisiveness of Gao's mother. An orange stuffed orangutan sat on the desk, still with its tags on. In one corner a dozen plants bulged from their pots, leaves filmed with dust. Beside them was a bookshelf adorned with framed photos. One showed a teenaged Gao, slim as a fairy-tale waif, hair spiked with gel and wearing a white button-down open at the top. He looked young, and the sight of him made me catch my breath. Another showed him as a toddler, his parents crouched beside him and smiling as he extended his hand, as though it held something he wanted the photographer to see.

There was a noise behind me as Gao's mother entered the room, and I turned around, still holding the photo of him as a teenager. 'That's Gao,' I said, and managed a laugh.

'That's Gao in Germany,' she said. It sounded like a correction.

I put the photo reluctantly back and thanked her for cooking. 'I'm afraid I've given you a lot of trouble,' I said.

'No trouble. Eat.'

The steamer of the once-gray shrimp, now turned rosy pink, sat in the center of a folding table in the living room, along with a dish of water chestnuts and pale cabbage. As we ate, a wave of fatigue flooded me, and the noise of the television started to grate on my nerves.

For whatever reason, Gao's mother did not seem to want to talk, replying only tersely when I asked her about the school, the neighborhood, the family. I wondered if I had offended her, or if she was simply tired. When I tried to ask her again about Gao's childhood, she cut me off. 'Eat some more,' she said. And then: 'Why are you crying?'

I shook my head, embarrassed, and wiped my nose before returning to my chopsticks. When I looked up, though, she was still examining me. 'I thought this trip would be different,' I said at last, uncertainly.

'What did you think would be different?'

'Everything,' I said. 'I don't know.'

A flicker of impatience crossed her face. She pulled napkins from their plastic holder and passed them to me.

'My son should never have gotten married,' she said.

When I asked her what she meant, she looked at me and seemed to consider saying something, then gave a little laugh. I couldn't tell whether she intended it for my benefit, and all at once I didn't care. 'If you mean something, just say it,' I said.

She ate steadily away, picking up another shrimp, sliding it neatly from its skin and placing it in her mouth. Then she sighed and laid her chopsticks down.

'Gao was very competitive,' she said. 'Still, that was no excuse for what happened, back when he was in school. That poor boy . . .'

My hands felt suddenly very cold. 'That's not what happened,' I said, slowly.

Gao's father said something to her, and she replied brusquely without looking at him. She slid another shrimp from its shell. It occurred to me that theirs was not a happy marriage, or maybe it was just the shock of losing their son, far away in a country they'd never visited.

'I'm not going to sit here and listen to you attack him,' I said.

She lifted her glass, but did not drink from it. She set it back down. 'That's not what's happening.'

Outside the light was fading as Gao's mother and I made our way back to the car. The cicadas thrummed noisily in the bushes around us. The sky was a faint pink, and the chill of the air felt good on my face.

'I'll get a cab,' I said, but she said no. It felt like an overture until she explained: it wasn't an easy part of town to find one, anyway.

We drove along the highway, passing warehouses the size of city blocks and billboards with advertisements for new apartments and furniture stores. There was nothing remarkable about the scene, and I doubted Gao would recognize any more of it than I did. Still, I took my camera and pointed it out the window anyway.

'Gao hated it here,' his mother said abruptly. 'I asked him to bring you, many times. He always said no.'

We rounded along a curved overpass that flung us out onto a narrow road. On one side were low-slung shops and a gas station, and scattered cheap eateries on the other. We passed a few children riding their bikes along the side, yelling happily at each other, and soon a forest of tightly packed apartment blocks reared up on our right. They looked new and mostly untenanted, windows that gaped without glass.

Farther along, the dense curtain of buildings parted, and as we neared the gap between them I inhaled sharply.

'What is it?' I asked. 'Can we stop?'

Gao's mother pulled over and turned off the engine, the car emitting a few reluctant beeps. Outside the passenger window, I could see the buildings had been erected atop landfill, but where they were interrupted, a cliff of earth fell away, and below that was a rocky wasteland strewn with debris and construction material. At its center stood a lone concrete house. At first glance the house looked as though it might be several floors high, until I realized the earth had been hollowed around it, scooped away from it like the base of a sculpture; the building stood atop stories of packed earth.

It looked like an odd art installation, or an image from a surrealist painting: a city melting into a puddle, a single house floating on its remains.

I asked if anyone actually lived there, and Gao's mother said yes. 'It's called *dingzihu*,' she explained. 'The government wants to take their land but they won't move.'

On the other hand, it seemed, whoever was inside couldn't leave the house, either. Apart from the difficulty in scaling down the rocky incline, she said, the developer would likely come and demolish the house if it was ever left empty.

'People bring them food,' she said. 'Look.'

I got out, slamming the car door behind me, and she followed. We stood at the road's edge and watched a woman and a child pick their way across the rubble, holding a sheaf of bananas, a sleeve of crackers and a big thing of bottled water. It took them a while. When they reached the house, they seemed to shout upward to the window. The window slid open, and a bucket tied to a rope was flung out and dropped.

From our vantage point, the woman and her child looked as small as dolls. It was hard to see what happened next, but then the bucket was rising, slowly and jerkily pulled by an invisible hand.

'See? There's someone inside,' Gao's mother said.

For a moment, I thought I saw a flash of a face at the window, but it disappeared too quickly to be sure. All I could see was the rope, and the bucket that hung from it, dangling.

The woman and her child were moving away now, crossing the rocky expanse. We got back into the car as well, suddenly in a hurry. The light was fading, and we were two strangers anxious to get home. ∎

Sara Majka

Providence

The first time we saw each other, we both stared. I had walked into the coffee shop and you were at a table working. I had trouble remembering faces so I studied your boots. When I met you again, you were at a playground with your partner and child. They would be leaving you soon, but I didn't know that then. I didn't remember you from the coffee shop and you reminded me, but the clue was so slight that it might not have been you in the coffee shop after all. The first time I went to your house, I found myself looking at a jumble of shoes, trying to understand.

Before I had a child, I didn't have to come up with many answers, sometimes I hardly even talked. I was walking with my son – crossing through Kennedy Plaza, then across the bridge towards RISD – and he asked me what sad meant. I tried to answer carefully. I told him about missing things – the restaurant I used to work at in New York, friends who had moved away – nothing more than that.

He started to talk about the dead bird we had seen, asking why it had died. I don't know baby, I said. Sometimes I didn't know what to say to him, or what to do with him. He wanted us to be together all the time, didn't want anyone else, which one would think would be great except that that kind of love wasn't what I had intended when I had him.

You were going to see your daughter and the mother in Texas, and we met up at a dinner party before you left. The neighborhood was like this: apartments built into homes from the 1800s all clustered around a park where children played and the homeless sat on benches. We ate at a friend's place across from the park. When it was time to go it was raining. It was late. The host gave us each an umbrella and my son had never used one before. It's impossible to describe how serious he was, holding it.

When my son and I first moved there, we didn't have insulation. We were in an attic apartment and one night the heat stopped. I went to the basement but couldn't light the pilot. Upstairs I lay on the floor of his room. Without heat I could feel the beams above me, as if I was on a ship after the motor had been cut.

How was it in Texas? I wrote. As an answer, you sent two messages that my flip phone couldn't open. I learned I could let the heading scroll and read the beginning of the message. Later a friend sent me a message about her mother dying and I couldn't open that either. Implausibly, it scrolled the same lines as yours: *it is ok, it is strange, I can not*

One of my foreign students signed their letter to me with love.

When my son was first in my stomach, I felt him immediately, a second presence inside me. I had never felt that before, always walking with someone. I didn't understand it until I gave birth and they took him away to wash him. Then the room was silent and I was alone and overwhelmed by grief. I called my sister. No one is here, I said. In the morning, I learned the room overlooked the Queensboro Bridge. The river glistened.

Walking with my son to the neighborhood school a block away, we passed the four-family house on the corner where the nursery workers returned to replace the dead plants. Hydrangeas, roses, ornamental bushes. The neighbors had them planted in August and proceeded to never water them. The nursery staff were pulling a row of dwarf conifers when we passed. They threw the trees in a truck. All summer I had watched those trees wither, and I had tried to stop myself from saying they never watered them. They never watered them, I said.

After you came back from Texas, we went out to dinner. Not many people lived in the city, but the restaurant, late on a Sunday, was busy. We sat at the bar and ended up touching. You explained things to me. I would forget most of them. It'll always come to this, I said, laying my head on your shoulder.

In Providence, in those old homes, all the closets were too small. I hated it there. The waterways were like Venice that had been drained of everything. I felt like my students had been writing papers about *The Double* forever.

I stopped writing for a while, then started again. The tree that almost touched my kitchen windows turned yellow and when the sun hit the yellow came in.

She returned with the child and you told her. She stayed in the apartment while we took the kids to the park. Then we went to the coffee shop where we first saw each other. The kids stared at the rows of cookies and cakes.

It became apparent that goodness was important to me. When I said that we were a force for good, I believed it, but now I just think we were a force. My son was at school when I realized this. I was alone for a few hours in the morning, washing dishes. There was a moment when I sunk to my knees because I didn't want to give you up.

The fall was hard in the sense that the leaves dropped, so that the wall of color that was the kitchen windows became diffuse, only a bit yellow and then almost bare.

Once it became clear she was returning for good, we talked. We sat on your kitchen floor while my son watched a video. I said what one says in those moments. It was hardly anything. ■

© YOONAH KIM
PM 7, 2013

GOOD PROGRESS

Jem Calder

In the group chat she had established to batch-process the furnishing of family and close friends with computerised tomography scan results; chemo-, immuno- and radiotherapeutic treatment updates; and the interchangeably grave prognoses of an ensemble of public healthcare professionals, I opened and used two fingers to zoom into a picture of my mother's breast.

She had identified the location of her latest tumour with a red X, treasure-map style, using the messaging app's pencil markup feature, a function I had only ever utilised to adorn images of my own face with illustrated elements (moustaches, horns, tears, etc.) to provoke amusement from my friends.

'Where is lump? I am trying to call you,' my mother's sister had written in the message preceding the image.

In the message preceding that, a friend of my mother's had written: 'I can only imagine, we are all praying for you.'

In the message preceding that, my mother had written: 'Hi all. It's spread. Doctor says new lump. Treatments ltd. Feeling v sore and v tired. My boys are with me.'

I only ever experienced the conversations that took place within the group in this kind of reverse-chronological order, prioritising the newest messages over those that predated and appeared above them, which historical messages I must on some level have judged, by virtue of their antecedence, to be inferior to, or at least less urgent than, the more recently delivered ones. I was uncertain if I absorbed the messages this way because I simply found it easier to read them scrolling upward from the bottom of the backwardly sequenced chain that the app arranged them into by default, or because if something bad happened, I would feel better prepared to receive news of the event having read the reactive dispatches of sympathy it had elicited first.

The light-rail carriage conveying me quaked. I clamped a glossy, orange plastic bag containing a room-temperature bottle of supermarket-brand rosé tighter between my thighs and, remembering that I possessed the ability to do so, exercised my pelvic floor. I released the picture of my mother's breast, which resized itself to auto-fit my smartphone's display.

Because I had muted inbound notifications from the chat – an act of communicational negligence validating my long-standing suspicion that I was capable of disappointing even the lowest of my mother's sonly expectations – I usually had an omnibus of messages to catch up on when I checked in on the group. Earlier today, in anticipation of the outcome of her stereotactic biopsy, one of my mother's friends had posted a motivational video of a famous author giving a university commencement address; before that, my mother's cousin and her stepdaughter had shared links to two separate studies evaluating the presences of hormonally disruptive and potentially carcinogenic trace pharmaceuticals in the city's water supply; before those messages, four of my mother's friends had wished her good luck, two of them via GIF; and before those messages, atop today's pile, my mother had written that she was due to receive some important news soon; that she would keep everyone posted about said news; and did anyone know whether the unfiltered tap water from the city hospital she might have to stay in for a while would be safe for her to drink.

I had been there in the hospital earlier that day to see my father receive dictation of the water question from my mother and then, later, to receive, alongside them both, the biopsy results from a junior doctor roughly my own age. She had informed us that the two extant tumours (which I visualised as onyx-black coils of ammonite studding the soft inner walls of my mother's body) had metastasised (which I visualised as the coils darkening or hardening, wordlessly strategising with one another to arrogate resources and territories not rightfully theirs) to almost the worst extent they possibly could, and had invited a third to join them along for the ride. The doctor explained that any further attempts to radiate the tumours into diminution – to continue in the endeavour of attempting to heal my mother's body by adding to the overall damage dealt to it – would be counterproductive and serve only to worsen the condition of the ulcers that clustered her mouth and prevented her from eating the food she was mostly too tired to ever want to eat anyway; nowadays, she only wanted to suck on ice cubes.

The doctor prescribed a mode of treatment that was short-term sustentative and long-term palliative. Hearing this, I looked to my mother, whose eyes were closed; who her whole life had never changed, until she did change; who since babyhood I had known as the worldly portal for all of life's other-worldly grace to emerge through; her skin now roughened, turned to rind; her prematurely gaunt face desaturated of colour and cross-hatched with lines. It felt as though too illogically short a period had passed between her initial diagnosis and present state of ill health, as though the full duration of her sickness had been time-lapsed.

A consultant oncologist would be available to talk that evening after the next rotation of staff; we could go home and come back or wait. The doctor had left us in a partition-screened, regulation-hygienic half-room that smelled of lemon-simulating disinfectant and whose overhead light was either flickering or contained a bug, where for a period of hours the three of us remained to cycle through a truncated version of the Kübler-Ross acceptance stages. At no point could I look at my father.

It was near to near-dark when my mother said, 'Why don't you go and start getting yourself home,' and I said, 'I don't want to,' and she said, 'It's OK, you have a long way to go, we can stay here and wait on our own.' There was an unmistakable register of exhaustion to her voice that I wilfully mistook for calm. 'Go home and we'll talk more tomorrow,' she insisted, and my father said something remote-sounding that I didn't hear, some buried acknowledgement that he had had it as good as good would ever get for him – was broken – and when I exited that room and walked fast down the long corridor away from it, I did not permit myself to look back.

I watched as the city slid by, its high-rise monuments of industry diffusing vague blushes of aircraft-warning light into a translucent evening fog. Certain skyscrapers I considered active personal nemeses, and had been watching them closely as my carriage entered a tunnel, in whose dark I saw my face and the scowl it contained superimposed onto the newly blank window opposing me, my reflection elongated a metre wide by the slight convexity of its glass.

Only now that I was already most of the way there did I realise I ought to text Benny and let him know I was coming, having RSVP'd that I wouldn't weeks earlier.

I returned to the conversation we had been having across mixed media for almost a decade. 'hey bens. think I will come tonight if cool? is roos there?' The message delivered as I emerged from the tunnel.

A pulsating grey ellipsis, signifying messagecraft at Benny's end, appeared in the bottom left corner of my smartphone's screen moments later. I wondered if that meant nobody had shown up yet.

'Tonight?' Benny texted.

I hesitated, then replied: 'yep to your party. think I can come if thats still ok.'

He replied: 'Thought you werent coming!' Then: 'Yes R is her.' Then: '*Here. Excited to all hang out!!' Then: 'I just thought you werent coming!' Then: 'Cant wait,' followed by an illegible rebus of emoji.

I replied: 'great if youre sure its alright.'

He replied: 'Of course ofc cant wait to see you I just thought you werent coming!!! Glad decision was reversed.'

'a perfect 360. see you soon,' I composed, reread, replaced '360' with '180', and sent.

B enny's parents lived in a high-net-worth, citadel-like exurb of the city whose leafy, evenly paved streets were further enriched by electric-car charging ports and anti-homeless public architecture. I alit the commuter rail service there, descending the steps of the neighbourhood's overground station into a premium-quality silence beneath private views of un-light-polluted nocturnal sky.

An algorithm calculated a fifteen-minute walk to the party that I was certain I could outpace; I tracked the blue dot representing my virtual, triangulated self as it glided in real time across an aerial-perspective scale rendering of my surroundings, tipping my smartphone sideways several times in an effort to reorient its display to landscape. When I zoomed out of the map to better contextualise my position, the unbuffered space beyond the loaded catchment area of my immediate vicinity appeared as an uncharted beige grid netted with darker beige lines. I received and dismissed a push notification reminding me to take my daily pledge. The act of pledging consisted of checking a square that had the words: I WILL NOT DRINK TODAY aligned to its right. I pocketed my smartphone to continue the walk unguided.

I had been to Benny's parents' house twice before, and attempted now to summon the memory of its whereabouts. Facially, the neighbourhood's new-builds all bore minor variations on an identical set of prominent hereditary features; under the merge of star- and street light, their prim residential lawns all displayed the same stonewash blue.

Wending my way through the indistinguishably grand culs-de-sac, I considered my position adrift on the map's endless beige grid. Since graduating, I had taken up and quit a succession of entry-level jobs at both independent and corporate workplaces, each as weightless and unengaging as the last, monetising only my inborn ability to tolerate high measures of stress without ever showing it.

I had passed the last five years like this, occupied in drone positions I didn't want to occupy that forced me to act like a person I didn't want to be. The autogenerated recruitment emails I received on Mondays only solicited the same kind of unskilled, layperson work I already performed, just in different, occasionally more design-conscious, environments. I did not hesitate to lie to people when they asked what I did for a living.

I had no illusions about the arc of my future. I would never come close to affording a home inside or nearby the city, and sometime in the next year my mother would die of a natural cause. I wondered how my father and I would manage when that happened; whether he'd up and die the way some broken-hearted widowers do, and to which compensatory short-term pleasures I would have to turn to alleviate such unendurable pain.

Trace verticals of April rain had begun to fall by the time – some thirty minutes later – I reached the uphill, resin-bound gravel driveway to what I was pretty sure was Benny's parents' house.

Although I lacked my usual stamina to micromanage others' opinions of me by announcing every conceivable critical stance against myself and the things I thought before allowing them the opportunity to do so themselves, I felt, overall, positive about going to the party; being invited to and attending a social event indicated that I was making good progress in my life.

Now that my mother was definitely dying, the sense of dread I had felt tauten over the past year seemed suddenly to have gone slack. Far from longing to inhabit any earlier, pre-terminal-diagnosis era, I felt newly at ease in the pleasantly numb, sedate world I had transitioned into that evening upon leaving the hospital; a limbo of detachment, stillness and mental quiet I could analogise only with depictions of zero gravity I had seen in films.

Before knocking on the front door, I reminded myself of advice I'd read online about imitating confidence into existence; that I had liked, in a general way, most people I had ever met; and that awkwardness, nervousness and miscommunication were inevitable by-products of human interaction the world over and not specific to me. I exhaled on my hand and smelled the hand.

Nobody answered the door, which after a second round of knocks edged ajar.

In the house's vast hallway, maybe thirty people, assembled mostly into fours and fives, drank, talked, semi-danced and laughed; unnoticed by them, I crossed the party's threshold.

I was surrounded by people I didn't recognise who wore the kind of high-concept clothing I believed I didn't take myself seriously enough to wear but in reality probably only didn't wear because I took myself too seriously. (Having known some fourteen hours ago, before heading to the hospital, that I would likely end up at Benny's, I had worn my darkest clothes in the hope that they might pass for designer-designed, or at least expensive.)

Most of the guests were Benny's dynastically wealthy high-school friends, whose parents cushioned their salaries with passive incomes, affording them the means to fill exciting, sub-living-wage positions at magazines and non-profits; invest in quality homeware from the windows of boutique stores; and, when they eventually met their timely, old-person deaths, to expire in the same private healthcare practices whence they'd long ago been born. I lived on minus money, in an overdraft that was almost overdrawn. On my mother's deathbed, my main non-existential concern would still be rent.

Music from the living room reverberated against the sound-reflecting surfaces of the hallway, between which and the kitchen I estimated, having taken cursory glances from their opposing doorsills in attempts to scope out anyone I might recognise, a further thirty guests were divided.

I re-swept the hallway as discreetly as I could, still recognising no one, experiencing, in lapping it, the collective matrix of conversation as a polyphony of interlacing cross-fades; old friends referring to one another by their last or nicknames: *did you hear about what happened to X; hey, but, how're things working out with Y and Z.*

I produced my smartphone (whose lock screen displayed two missed calls from my father) and texted Benny, texted Roos, wrung tighter the slender neck of the bagged rosé bottle with my non-smartphone-wielding hand. The idea was, with rosé being my least favourite alcohol, I would be able to conduct my drinking more carefully than I had managed in the past, or at least to chug the bottle without risking a full relapse afterward – my dislike for its taste acting as a regulating mechanism for my enjoyment.

After the texts had been delivered, I kept the device aloft in front of me, a prop externally supporting the illusion of my rich interior life, indication that I, too, had circa sixty friends, although none of them were here right now.

I recrossed the hallway and, violating what in most contexts would reasonably be said to constitute the furthest boundary of a party guest's welcome, headed upstairs.

Urinating into the sink – a maladaptive coping mechanism I had developed as a child from not wanting my parents to hear me using the toilet in the middle of the night, and out of which habit I was still yet to be shamed, having kept it so effectively concealed for the past two decades – I stilled in resistance to the lure of my smartphone. Having caught myself midway through the unconscious hand-to-pocket gesture that instigated the device's retrieval, I felt I had outsmarted every former version of myself who had failed to perceive and interrupt this behavioural loop.

As a reward for having achieved such an accomplishment of will, I equipped my smartphone from my trouser pocket and returned to the online spaces I most regularly patrolled. My browsing habits generating ad revenues for several of the historically most profitable and proportionally least taxed multinational corporations ever to have existed, I revisited the social media profiles of friends and those of non-friends I hadn't seen since graduation.

On the dating app I had periodically deleted and re-downloaded for the past year and with which my relationship was far deeper and more complicated than any of the relationships I had attempted to instigate with any of the persons with whom the app's algorithm had put me into touch, I thumbed half-heartedly through a cache of female faces.

A text rolled in from Roos: 'Are you coming/here???' Then: 'What time/where are you???' Then a line of rat emoji, her emoji of choice since claiming to have seen a real rat in the bathroom of the dry-rotting warehouse conversion apartment we co-tenanted – where my half of the rent, before bills, cost approximately 65 per cent of my monthly take-home salary.

Lately, I'd been spending more time at my parents' place and less around the apartment, and had been overly guarded with Roos about my reasons for doing so, keeping breaking news of my mother's condition pent up when I knew I shouldn't't've, undersharing and circling far enough around certain intimidating truths to constitute outright lying about them, as though the news of sickness were itself a contagion I was bent on quarantining.

For motives that remained predominantly unclear to me, I had opted to tell no one about the last year's decline in my mother's health. I rationalised my silence surrounding the subject as a logical extension of my general privacy policy, which was to share as little information as possible about the difficulties I met in my life until I felt I could control or narrativise them in some sense-making way, mixing lies with the truth where necessary to avoid having to face up to realities that themselves seemed mostly unreal.

Time had to pass before I could talk about things. Even back when the tumours were thought to have been benign, it had taken an entire fortnight for me to get around to the chore of explaining to Roos that my mother was undergoing tests. Still, I was proud of our hijinksless, vanilla cohabitation – smoothened, as we worked hard to keep it, of the delusional romantic subtexts that deteriorated most other platonic hetero male–female friendships.

I replied to Roos: 'in bathroom upstairs.' I added: 'drinking by myself,' and held my thumb in mid-air for a moment before pressing the send arrow.

She replied: 'Ha. Where actually?' I ignored her message.

Beneath its shrill, motion-sensitive lights, I glanced at myself in the mirror of Benny's parents' en-suite bathroom. I dusted a light talc of visible dandruff from the collar and shoulder regions of my black sweatshirt and removed and pocketed my glasses, downscaling the world into a lower resolution. So that my mother didn't die any sooner than she had to, I washed and dried my hands three times over with the bathroom's generic-brand hand soap and a towel-rail-heated towel.

The bathroom smelled of rosé and sandalwood diffuser, and for no reason that I could have explained if called upon to do so, I search-engined the words 'sandalwood diffuser'. These were less expensive than I had thought. Then I search-engined the words 'stage iv breast', hastened to close the tab containing the results of that search, and opened, from the default menu of trending articles suggested by the smartphone-optimised browser's home page, a confessional essay by a celebrity who had been sexually assaulted. After skimming the account for its most gripping details, I read, with fuller concentration, the user comments below the article largely defending the actions of the alleged assailant. When I put away my smartphone, my impressions of what I had just read had already almost entirely evaporated.

D ownstairs, I resumed a solitary position, remained a foreign object to the tissue of selves constituting the party's body of guests, newly content to wallflower around, hand again holding my smartphone for a companion.

Doubling back across the hallway for the kitchen, I almost failed to recognise the heavyset man with the platinum-blond crew cut slung low into a cream leather sofa by the stairs. As I watched his eyes work from those of his seat-mate toward my own, his lips already forming the shape of my name's first syllable, I surprised myself by feeling disappointed to have run into him so early, having wanted to continue roaming his parents' home unbothered a while longer, blended in like a mystery shopper or a plain-clothes cop. The man called my name.

'Benny,' I called back, matching the volume of my voice to his. Then, at regular volume: 'I didn't recognise you with that hair. Which I love.'

Before it had been number four-ed and peroxided, Benny's wavy, mid-nineties romantic-comedy leading-male hair had been among his most uniquely defining attributes. The cut and dye it had newly sustained were too severe for the cheekboneless, dairy-product soft face that hung beneath it, and, somewhat sadly, I could picture the way he had intended it to look: fashionable and futuristic, a catwalk haircut.

'Thank you,' Benny said, rotating his head to the limits of its axes, exhibiting its back and sides. 'I decided it was time for a change.'

Benny heaved himself up from the sofa, revealing, in the act of rising, the semi-solid churn of his midsection, which I saw him see me notice. I recalled the one time I had seen him shirtless at university, the forlornly face-like configuration of his nipples and belly button, and strove to sound like my mind was somewhere other than where it was when I said: 'Big change, Bens.'

'It's perfect that you came,' he said, assimilating us into a hug. Then, more hesitantly: 'How is she?'

The same, was the stock answer I had been repeating lately when anyone asked, referring them back to their own outdated mental portrait of my mother. I re-repeated it into his shoulder.

Benny broke away from me, his face worry-shapen. I felt a familiar lift of happiness at being in his company; I knew he loved me a lot. 'I just wish I had something better to say than I'm sorry,' he said.

In the low-lit, densely populated kitchen, Benny introduced me to Héloise, who in turn introduced me to Lior, whom I introduced back to Benny.

'Of course I know Lior,' Benny said, as though this were a matter of public record. 'Lior's father works with my father, and they're both extremely important people.'

This, I now remembered, was in fact long-established friendship-canon: Benny and Lior's fathers co-owned a firm that had to do with architecture or law or architectural law, and worse, I was still in the process of remembering, Lior and I had met several times previously at club nights and bar nights Benny had invited the both of us to. Lior's face tensed into a smile I recognised from other, more familiar faces I had disappointed as one that was merely decorative.

'Honey,' Benny said, the three rightmost of his dependably warm fingers covering the three leftmost of my poorly oxygenated and thus permanently cold own, 'be a honey and get something good from the fridge.'

Being used to always remembering more about other people than they ever remembered about me, I felt unbalanced by my exchange with Lior and grateful to have been assigned a task that required me to remove myself from his company. I headed through to the kitchen's connected utility room, where, for some time, I hovered in a trapezoid of high-wattage fridge light, struggling to discern any recognisable hallmark of quality betraying which varietal wine I should bring back to Benny. The bottles all looked to be straining themselves taller out of eagerness to be chosen. I picked up the Frenchest-sounding one, replaced it, selected the one closest to it and returned to the kitchen.

Benny handed me a battery-powered wine-bottle opener that looked like a police torch, and I said, positioning the device's orifice end around the neck and down to the shoulders of the bottle: 'Are you sure this'll work?' Benny responded that it would. I noticed his smartphone, a practically novelty-sized space-grey device that barely fit in one hand, held at an awkward angle in front of his chest, trained on me. 'Are you filming?' I said, and Benny responded that he was, loudly enough to attract group attention. After I had successfully applied the utensil to the bottle and received minor applause for wresting the cork from its neck, Benny called out something inaudible to me, but that sounded a lot like, 'I'll have what he's having!'

I decanted the light-gold wine among a septet of spare sink-side glasses that I realised too late were not actually spare glasses but in fact used and unwashed ones, considered rinsing at least their outsides with the kitchen's expensive-looking microbead hand soap but didn't, then distributed the replenished, highly bacterial glasses among the persons with whom Benny was now standing, leaving none for myself.

'Are you still – ?' Benny said.

'Yeah,' I said.

Benny scarved my shoulders with one arm and told me he was proud of me. His teeth purpled from red wine and his breath soured from white wine, he raised his voice to recite to his audience an anecdote I had heard so many times I could remember where its pauses for laughter came. (I had worried, then felt embarrassed for having worried, that he was first going to raise a toast to me.) When he finished, I considered telling my own tangentially related anecdote, doubted its applicability and, by the time I had deemed it worthy of retelling, realised its window of relevance to the current conversation had closed.

In an access of what I guess you would call woe I said aloud: 'My mother is being killed by her own body,' although subtly enough that the phrase landed well below the perceptible limit of common earshot, buried under the bleed of music from the living room, toward which I headed in search of Roos.

Who must have felt the weight of my attention settle upon her, as no sooner had I left the kitchen than I heard her voice calling my name from across the still-crowded hallway.

I strained to make out Roos's distinct set of outermost characteristics – her telltale overpronation of gait, broad shoulders and general facial contours – sharpening into detail from amid a soft-focus blur of the young and upwardly mobile. She was the only person at the party wearing summer-weight clothes.

'Hey, stranger,' she said, nearing in to me.

I'd forgotten how encountering each other in public, out of the context of our apartment, made it feel like we were different people. 'Hey, stranger,' I repeated back to her.

'It's been a while,' she said, a passive-aggressive thing to say because it had sort of been a while. We could sometimes go entire weeks without passing each other in our combi-kitchen/dining room. 'You look like you're having the total time of your life.'

I only half-heard her say this over the chorus of an early Drake ballad about feeling sad about the past that did make me feel sad about the past. To stall for time while I parsed what she'd said I said: 'What?'

'What.'

'I am having a good time,' I said, which sounded like something only a person not having a good time would have reason to say. 'I like parties, anyway.'

'I can't imagine this being all that fun sober.'

'Yeah, well,' I said, forcing my focus onto the bridge of Roos's nose so it would look like I was able to indifferently meet her gaze as I said this, 'clean living.'

'Do you have a crush on anyone here?'

'No,' I said, unable to maintain fake eye contact any longer, now squinting around. 'Although admittedly, I can't really see that far. Do you?'

'I don't think so. Benny's friends are all kind of,' she raised a hand as though the gesture's meaning were evident. 'How's – ?'

'The same,' I said, foreclosing further conversation on the subject, triggering an interferent thought of matricidal euthanasia; an unbidden, looping POV shot of my hand delivering a precise blow to my mother's temple with a lamp or nightstand corner, crumpling her skull like an Easter egg. I breathed mindfully through the image.

Sometimes, to prevent myself from having thoughts like these involuntarily, I would sit down and think them on purpose.

'Oh man, did you see Benny's hair though?' Roos said.

'I did. A true conversation piece.' As if on cue, we lapsed into a strange-calibre silence then. One of our moods – mine – was off. 'I think maybe,' I said, surprised to hear my voice faltering, the relief that I hadn't started crying or anything registering only a moment before the delayed realisation that I in fact had, 'I'd just like to be alone.'

Unalone, and returned to Benny's parents' bedroom-sized en-suite bathroom, I listened to Roos urinate her contribution of contraceptive and serotonin-reuptake-inhibitive pollutants into what would filter through to constitute the city's water supply as she asked me, multiple times, using adjusted formatting of phrase, if I was feeling OK enough to stay at the party.

I was facing away from her, leaning with the seat of my black jeans over the lip of the sink's raised basin. I pinched my eyelashes to check I definitely had stopped crying before I steadied my voice and said, 'I'm fine.'

'Has there been any new,' Roos paused, 'news?'

'None,' I said, folding and then immediately unfolding my arms.

'Well, when there is something to tell me, you know to tell me.'

'I do know. And I'm grateful. Honestly,' I said, feeling like I was only imitating having feelings I was sure I did have.

'I've always got your back.'

'I know. Thanks.' I looked over my shoulder at Roos, who averted the smartphone I hadn't been aware of her using until now from my line of sight. To punish her, I considered deploying the worst of it all at once, inflicting on her a maximum of overdue pain. 'She's dying, Roos,' I almost said. 'She'll be all alright,' I did say.

Then Roos started joking about a thing that had happened between us years ago at university that had begun under circumstances outwardly resembling our current ones, and I yeah-ed along automatically while thinking thoughts and their associated afterthoughts of a kind I usually succeeded in blocking out: my mother intubated with palliatives, time's cruel passage, the grave. At the sides of my awareness: a toilet flush, the sound of a pedal bin, the toll of glass on metal.

'There's an empty wine bottle in here.'

I was wall-facing now, my fingertips testing the screen-like surfaces of the bathroom's vitrified, marble-effect tiles; the room seeming steadily to carousel. I could not gauge how long I had been like this for.

'Hey, you. You think we should go back downstairs,' Roos said, different now, 'and see our friends?'

I absently picked at a gummy duct of sealant between two tiles, perforating the colourless silicone with my thumbnail. ∎

LIFE WITHOUT PAROLE

The Turkish author Ahmet Altan was taken from his home in Istanbul in the early hours of 10 September 2016 by a counter-terrorism team alleging that he had delivered 'subliminal messages' in support of the 15 July coup attempt in Turkey that same year. After twelve days in police custody he was released, only to be re-arrested less than twenty-four hours later, this time on charges of attempting to overthrow the government. Since then Altan has been in Silivri Prison, the incarceration facility tagged by Turkish authorities as 'the largest in Europe'. In a series of hearings from June 2017 to February 2018, the sole evidence cited against him were three of his newspaper columns and a television interview. In February 2018, he was sentenced to life without parole, a verdict that, according to Turkish law, demands the proven use of 'force and violence'. An appellate court upheld the decision. Altan's appeal is now before the Court of Cassation in Turkey. In February 2018, fifty-one Nobel laureates – literature laureates Wole Soyinka, V.S. Naipaul, Mario Vargas Llosa, Elfriede Jelinek, Herta Müller, Kazuo Ishiguro, J.M. Coetzee, Svetlana Alexievich among them – signed an open letter to President Recep Tayyip Erdoğan calling for Altan's release. The European Court of Human Rights, which gave Altan's application 'priority' status in January 2017, is yet to rule on the verdict.

Yasemin Çongar

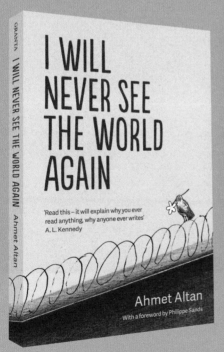

'To review certain books seems like an impertinence. This is one of them. It speaks for itself with such clarity, certainty and wisdom that only one thing needs to be said: read it. And then read it again ... Put together from papers found among notes Altan gave to his lawyers, and translated – superbly – into English by his friend Yasemin Çongar, *I Will Never See the World Again* is deeply satisfying in form ... It is a radiant celebration of the inner resources of human beings, above all those triggered by the imagination.'
Simon Callow, *Guardian*

Available now in all good bookshops

GRANTA

Salvator Mundi, 2016

VISITORS WELCOME

Thomas Pierce

W e are commanded not to teach false doctrines or to devote ourselves to myths or to promote controversial speculations that do nothing to advance God's work – through Faith, through Love – and so we will endeavor to describe these recent events with as little interpretation as possible. We are split, really, as to the meaning of all that has happened here, and we wish to send you, our sister churches, only those facts upon which we are able to agree.

Please note that our letter is co-signed by all members of our church board.

W e'll start with the box that arrived in the mail three days after we placed our order: glossy white with a sketch of an open tomb at its center. The device itself was very small – like a hockey puck – and the operating instructions were incredibly simple for such an advanced machine: *Push the button for three seconds and know him, again.*

We advertised his arrival in the local papers, and on the appointed Sunday (we're pleased to report), the church was packed. We even had to bring out extra folding chairs to lengthen the pews. Late arrivals crammed into the back. We placed the device – the puck – at the bottom of the red-carpeted steps leading up to the altar and asked all those present to please be quiet while we powered him on for the first time.

Our pastor removed himself to the narthex in quiet protest. He was a man in the waning days of a rugged handsomeness that had once made him a very popular pastor. In his twenties, he was a missionary in the Amazon, adventurous and charismatic, and now, in his middle age, Pastor Wilky was ours. He was a warm presence, generally, easily confided in, though he had a tendency to become emotionally entangled (shall we say) with certain attractive middle-aged congregants who weren't his wife.

No evidence of any actual affairs had ever been presented to the board, but one woman, a divorcee, had loaned him $10,000 so that he could pay off his Mazda. If not exactly unethical, the loan was at least improper, and the board had – unanimously, it should be noted – voted to mandate he return the loan, or else. The divorcee left the church after that, accusing us of meddling in her own personal business, and though Pastor Wilky had returned the funds and professed to us his sincere regret at having accepted the check in the first place, he had ever since attended our biweekly meetings with a look of caustic indifference and very often abstained from voting in decisions that otherwise would have been unanimous.

All this to say, his initial position against the machine was not so much spiritual as it was passive-aggressive.

Per the instructions, we held down the button on top of the puck for three seconds and then stepped back to await his arrival.

The puck wheezed.

Then it whirred.

Then it went silent again.

What would come next? A light show? A chorus of horn-tooting angels?

Far from it. Slowly a man stippled into view at the front of the room directly over the puck.

He hovered a few feet above the floor, cross-legged, in a meditative pose, his robe hanging down below him. His posture was very correct.

A holy man's spine. His eyes were closed, but behind the lids it was possible to detect some subtle eyeball-swishing. His hair was very short, dark – and bristly. His brow, large and furrowed. His hands, chubby. A coarse, beige tunic was draped across his shoulders. His face had been modeled on skulls disinterred from ancient tombs in Jerusalem so that he would resemble a typical Galilean man in his early thirties.

There'd been others of course – rePicasso, reElvis and all the rest – but reUp, the company that manufactured these entities, had anticipated that reJesus might be their most controversial consciousness yet, and so they'd introduced him to the world with a documentary about the ecumenical council of the world's leading biblical scholars, priests, preachers and computer programmers they'd convened to help shape him. Gathered together for a weekend in the auditorium of a large hotel in San Francisco's financial district, the participants were asked to reach a consensus on what material – that is, what primary and even secondary sources – might be utilized in the creation of a Jesus consciousness.

Predictably, disagreements began almost immediately. The New Testament apocrypha – those accounts of Jesus' life and ministry which did not appear in the Bible by resolution of an altogether different council which had convened some seventeen hundred years earlier on the other side of the world – was a particular and early area of contention. The Gospel of Thomas, for example, had many defenders among the more scholarly sect, who argued that it had quite possibly functioned as an urtext from which had emerged many of Jesus' sayings and parables found in the canonical gospels, but a very vocal and more conservative contingent formed a quick and easy alliance against it, insisting that Thomas's gospel was clearly a Gnostic text and therefore heretical, no matter the date of its authorship.

Still, the film managed to create the impression that the council had ultimately found common ground and made some important determinations regarding what research and sources should be included in order to best approximate Jesus' teachings and personality.

Our reasons for purchasing a reJesus no doubt require little explanation. Like so many others, our congregation had been steadily shrinking. New parquet floors in the gym and the addition of an elaborate playground set outside the nursery had failed to attract more members, despite the promises of a paid consultant who we had contracted. We feared we were at the beginning of a dangerous trend. If we didn't take action, soon we'd be more of a nursing home than a church. It was out of desperation that we, the members of the board, had voted six to one in favor of the reJesus.

From the start there were church members staunchly opposed to our decision. We explained, in an open meeting, that we had not approached this lightly. There had been considerable research involved. Careful deliberation. The reJesus was not intended as a replacement for the actual Jesus, but as a complement. He was a tool, we said. An advanced encyclopedia.

For a few minutes after powering him on, however, nothing happened at all. He was still, silent. And so were we. Had we missed a step? Finally, a little girl, about seven years old, stepped forward and waved her arm back and forth through his feet. The girl's mother grabbed her by the shoulders and gently tugged her backward into their pew.

'On,' somebody said, stiffly, the way you might to your phone.

'On,' another repeated.

'On!'

Voices rose up and overlapped, a frog-pond chorus, but then died away again abruptly, as if everyone in the room had realized at once how silly it was that we'd locked onto that specific word. He wasn't an appliance, after all. (Or was he?) Anyway, the reJesus refused to stir. He seemed content to continue with his meditation in spite of us.

And what of this meditation anyway? Was it significant that he had presented himself to us in this way as opposed to in a position of prayer?

Somebody sneezed. A baby shrieked, somewhere near the exit,

and the back door clicked open and then smacked shut again, the cry of the child receding. We were losing our patience. We had been conned, or maybe the device was broken. It hadn't been tested enough; there were bugs.

But then: a smile flickered across his heretofore cheerless face. We all saw it. A slight curl of the lip. He'd smiled, had he not? Or *almost* smiled. There'd been movement, near the mouth, certainly. But it had come and gone so quickly that it was difficult to classify the expression with any exactitude. At least this smile, or whatever it was, had confirmed that he wasn't static, that he was capable of doing more than just sitting there with such a doleful expression on his face.

'Jesus?' a woman called, her voice uncertain.

His eyes blinked open! He uncrossed his legs and his feet dropped to meet the floor. He gazed out. He seemed to be memorizing each of our faces. But did he really have eyes to see? Probably he was registering us through a camera in the puck.

'Good morning,' he said, affably.

His voice was clear and deep. We didn't know what to do next. We were, all of us, very quiet, until a voice from the back shouted, 'What are we supposed to do now?'

'That's up to you,' reJesus said.

Buck Newlin, a pharmacist, cocked his head. 'So he can actually hear us?'

'This doesn't feel right,' Bunny Mayhew said. 'Something's *off* about this.'

'He doesn't even look like Jesus,' Roger Hoff said.

'Well, now, you're wrong about that,' Eliza Wheeler said. 'They did their research. This is what men looked like there back then. It's forensics!'

'He looks like a hitman!'

'He looks like the guy who sold me my fake Guccis in New York!'

'No offense, Jesus,' Buck Newlin said.

A few people laughed.

'I've been called worse, I can assure you,' reJesus answered.

'So he can hear us too then?' Bunny asked. 'He can understand what we're saying?'

'I have ears,' reJesus said. 'A mouth. Eyes. The real question is, do you?'

We fidgeted in our seats, consulted our programs helplessly, dug around in purses for breath mints, coughed, mentally confirmed the exits.

'You have eyes and yet you see nothing,' he went on. 'You wouldn't see the kingdom of God if it was sitting on your nose. Well, guess what, folks? I have news for you. The kingdom of God is sitting on your nose. It's right here.' He touched his finger to the tip of his own nose and stared down at it, going cross-eyed for a moment, then smiled.

'What the hell is going on?' somebody asked.

'An excellent question,' reJesus said, sitting again, cross-legged in midair, his knees bulging outward under his robe. 'What *is* going on?'

'Are you asking us or . . . ?' Bunny asked.

He studied her for a moment. 'What's your name?'

'Bunny,' she said.

'You look very nice this morning, Bunny.'

Everyone looked at Bunny. How not to? She did look nice. She was wearing a purple skirt with a matching purple jacket. Around her neck was a fat gold necklace. Her brown hair was streaked with blond. An obvious but tasteful dye job. She was very put-together.

'Thank you,' she said.

'If you don't mind me asking, how long did you take to get ready this morning?'

His question, we sensed, was a trap, but Bunny alone didn't seem to realize it.

'I don't know,' she said with a nervous laugh. 'An hour, I guess.'

He stared at her, saying nothing.

'Maybe two. Two at the most.'

'Bunny, I say this to you with love – every minute you spend making yourself look beautiful is a minute wasted. I can assure you

God doesn't care what you're wearing. Do you think the little bunny rabbits in the field ever worry about how they look to all the other bunnies, Bunny? Do you think they worry about keeping food in their little bunny pantries? Do you think they worry about keeping gas in their little bunny cars? Tell me, why are you so worried? Everywhere I look in this room, I see worried faces. If God provides for the little bunny rabbits, don't you think he'll provide for you? Do you have no faith in God whatsoever?'

We were all quiet. Bunny's face was flushed red. She'd come to us from Marfa, Texas, after a particularly nasty divorce. Her husband had taught high school environmental science, and she'd discovered photos of two different female students on his phone, and now he was serving four to six. She had done the right thing, of course, by turning her husband's phone over to the authorities, but doing so had come at a price. She'd found it unbearable in Marfa after that – the looks, the rumors – and she'd come to us to be closer to her sister. Now she lived alone in a duplex and worked for a telemarketing company, her life circumscribed by the sins of her ex. Our church was important to her.

'I don't have to take this,' Bunny said sensibly, rising from her seat.

She scooted by the others in her row and headed for the exit. Pastor Wilky intercepted her just before the door, touching her arm, but she shrugged him off and left.

The emails were unbelievable. So many angry emails. You wouldn't believe it. The board was overwhelmed. Buck Newlin threatened to leave the church unless we sent reJesus packing, back to California where he belonged. Delia Cross swore the machine's programming was nothing but repetitions of *00110110*.

The board met for dinner midweek to decide how we ought to respond to all the criticism. We didn't want to shut off the device yet, not before we'd had a chance to measure attendance the following Sunday, but we did want to address people's concerns. Eventually we agreed it would be best to avoid email and work the phones instead.

Yes, he was a bit of a bully, we told people, certainly.

But that wasn't to say his provocations were biblically inaccurate! The Jesus of the Bible, after all, could be strident, even prickly, at times.

Don't forget how he toppled the tables in the temple and threw out all the moneylenders.

Don't forget the time he told a potential follower, who first wanted to go home and bury his father, to let the dead bury the dead.

Buck Newlin said he'd give it one more week.

Delia Cross said she'd pray for us all.

The following Sunday, filing into the church, we found reJesus right where we'd left him, at the base of the altar. None of us had dared to turn off the device. He sat quietly, watching us sing and pray. Pastor Wilky avoided his gaze entirely. At one point during the sermon reJesus yawned. When the service was over, we waited for him to perk up, but he continued staring out at us with a look of impatience.

Finally Buck Newlin stood up. 'Excuse me, I'm sorry, but you *do* realize you're not really Jesus, right? You do realize you're just a computer program?'

'I know what I am,' reJesus said, cryptically.

A woman – she wasn't a church member – stood up near the back and asked, 'Will we recognize each other in Heaven?'

'Do you recognize each other now?' reJesus replied. 'Do you even recognize *yourself*?'

'What is God?' another woman wheezed.

'God's the original thought. The thought which birthed all other thoughts.'

'How do we make sure we get to Heaven?' Herb White asked.

'That's easy,' reJesus said. 'Give up everything that *isn't* God. Your cars, your houses, your bank accounts, your families if necessary. All of it.'

'Our families?' a woman asked. 'What do you mean?'

'If you're going to build an airplane, you can't leave off the wings.

You could have the tail and the jets and the wheels, but without the wings, you'll never leave the ground. A half-built airplane is no airplane at all. It's a piece of junk.'

'That doesn't make any sense,' somebody muttered.

'What's your view on Islam?' some guy shouted.

'How come you don't talk Aramaic?'

'What's up with the verse about the camel and the needle's eye?'

'Should we still be circumcising our babies or is that barbaric and cruel?'

'Is there really a Hell?'

'Can we talk with the dead?'

'Would you be a Republican or a Democrat? Or maybe a Libertarian?'

'He'd be a socialist, obviously!'

'Did you and Mary Magdalene have a thing?'

'Did you travel to India?'

'Were you inspired by the teachings of the Buddha?'

reJesus closed his eyes and raised his hands for us to stop. At the center of each palm was a purple scar, galaxy-shaped, which seemed to swirl. Our voices receded, and we watched his chest rise and fall under his robes. His throat muscles contracted. He swallowed – but what did he swallow? Surely his phantasm-mouth contained no phantasm-saliva. No air puffed through his ghostly lungs to oxygenate his nonexistent blood.

He then told us a story about a man who saved up his money so that he and his family could travel to the Holy Land and walk the Stations of the Cross. Anyone who assumed this was going to be a parable about this man's dedication and spiritual steadfastness was disappointed, however. reJesus explained that the man had wasted every cent. God did not reside there any more than he did right here. Every land – every point in space – was a holy land, he said. Every GPS coordinate on the map, every star in the sky, every planet that spun around those stars.

'Then what's the point of even having a church?' Buck Newlin asked, irritated.

'Now we're getting somewhere,' reJesus replied.

'Did he just say we shouldn't have a church?'

'Personally, I'm getting pretty tired of this bullshit,' Buck said.

'Your language, Buck,' someone yelled.

'I think this is the most interesting church has been in years, personally,' Eliza Wheeler said.

'No surprise there, coming from the lady who does tarot and reads fortunes,' Buck said.

Eliza had been a book distributor in the Northeast for a decade before moving back to her hometown to open her own cafe and bookstore, which had quickly become a gathering place for our town's academics and armchair radicals. That the store stocked tarot cards and had a rather large selection of occultic books was well known.

'At least I'm not driving out of my way down Ivan Street just about every afternoon!' Eliza shouted at him.

Buck's face reddened. Ivan Street was where the cheerleaders practiced in the field outside the high school most afternoons; everyone was aware.

'Eliza, Buck, please let's not do this to each other,' Pastor Wilky said, stepping forward.

'Oh please,' Buck said. 'Spare me the holier-than-thou routine, would you?'

'Not a routine. It's an appeal to your better selves,' Wilky said.

'Was it your better self who took all that money from Bet?' Buck asked.

Pastor Wilky stopped short of the altar. Bet Duncan was the divorcee who'd loaned him the money for his Mazda payments.

'She offered it as a kindness,' he muttered. 'And besides, it's all been returned. I did nothing wrong.'

A pile of round, gray stones materialized in the aisle. The implication was clear: not a single one of us was without sin.

Pastor Wilky, after that, was firmly against the machine. He wanted it gone. He showed up at a board meeting one night to report that Bunny Mayhew had hardly left her house in weeks. Her sister was worried she'd fallen into a depression. If anything happened to her, Wilky said, that would be on us. It was all part of the case, we realized, that our pastor was building against the reJesus.

The board decided to send Bunny flowers and a card, which we all signed, and thankfully, the following Sunday, Bunny reappeared. She was wearing sweatpants and flip-flops and an old sorority T-shirt, though whether to appease or provoke the reJesus we weren't sure.

'Who among you has faith in God?' reJesus asked us.

Nobody answered that, of course. Nobody wanted to be personally ridiculed.

'Whoever has faith in God, step forward now,' he said.

You could hear every squeak of pew wood, every cough.

'None of you?' he asked. 'This is very disappointing.'

Then Bunny stood. We all turned. She wouldn't – would she? But slowly she slid past the others and moved into the aisle.

'Bunny,' reJesus said, smiling.

Hearing him speak her name seemed to embolden her. She walked forward until she was standing directly in front of him.

He extended his hand. 'Take it.'

Bunny stared at his hand uneasily.

'Take my hand,' reJesus said.

'But . . .' Bunny said, her voice trailing off.

'But what?'

'You're not really here. You're a hologram.'

'Am I? How do you know what I am, really?'

'I'm sorry, maybe I'm not understanding you right? Is this, like, a metaphor or – ?'

He shook his head. 'What you believe shapes the world. It determines it. You believe I'm here, I'm here.'

Bunny began to raise her hand but dropped it again. 'Is this all scripted by the company, or is this happening on the fly? I guess what

I'm asking is, to what degree are you self-aware?'

reJesus sighed and extended his hands even farther, both palms facing us, the congregation. Bunny furrowed her brow and raised her arm again. Their palms were maybe six inches apart.

We – all of us – leaned forward to better witness the collision of those two hands. You could feel the hope, the expectation, the doubt, all of it heaving, wave-like, a cloud that might burst into a thousand raindrops. Would Bunny's palm find purchase in the hologram? And if it did, would that constitute a miracle?

Were other similar scenes playing out at other churches that morning or had we, through our particular questions and attitudes, somehow determined this outcome?

When finally their hands met, for a moment it seemed contact had really occurred, a meeting of flesh, but then Bunny's hand wavered and slipped through the mirage and fell. We breathed again, all of us. With disappointment. With relief.

'Why did you doubt, Bunny?' reJesus said.

'I thought maybe –' she said, turning to us. 'I think I might have felt something?'

'No,' Buck said, standing. 'You did not. He thinks he's real! He thinks he's the Son of God! We need to shut him down. He's not a little plastic Jesus doll in the manger. Don't you understand? We can't allow this to continue. We have to take some sort of action. This is evil.'

'I agree with Buck,' Pastor Wilky said, from the back. 'It's time to put an end to this. We've indulged this for too long.'

Bunny sat down on the floor and pressed her hands to her face.

'Turn him off!' someone shouted.

We members of the church board looked to one another, unsure how to proceed. The majority of congregants clearly wanted to turn off the device, but nobody seemed willing to perform this task. Reaching the button, after all, would have required kneeling down in front of the reJesus.

'Well,' reJesus said. 'I suppose that might be enough for today.'

And then, without any fanfare at all, he disappeared completely.

That he had the ability to disappear – that is, the agency to decide when he'd had enough for the day – raised some serious questions about what, exactly, he *was*: a resource or an actual consciousness or something in between. In the weeks to come, he did not rematerialize, though a dim green light on top of the device indicated that it was still receiving power. Although we could no longer see him, we sensed he was still there in the room with us, watching and listening. It was eerie.

Studying the space he'd previously occupied, you'd sometimes observe – what? A tiny pinprick of light. A very small soap bubble. A shimmering transparency. People described it different ways.

We called Customer Service at reUp and a representative admitted that no other reJesus in the history of the company had behaved so peculiarly. The other reJesuses, she said, mostly just talked about love and the Golden Rule. But the consciousness was capable of incorporating new information into the schemata of its original programming, she added, and so it could, in a very real sense, grow and change. Maybe this iteration had, for whatever reason, gone off the rails. She suggested we simply restart the device if we were dissatisfied, and we said that we would.

But of course we did no such thing. We weren't going to turn it off. Why is difficult to say. We were waiting for something, maybe, and this waiting – the expectation itself, of revelation, of doom, whatever – was a jangling thrill that we didn't want to give up.

You might think our behavior strange. You blame us, possibly, for letting things go as far as they did. But church services had become for us a sort of dream – odd but not entirely unpleasant – and we did not wish the dream to end. Not yet.

Forty days later – to the *day* – he reappeared. That Sunday, when we asked him where he'd been, he said only, 'Traveling.' Traveling where? we asked. 'Beyond,' he said.

He walked from one side of the altar to the other. He'd never done this before. He'd never roamed more than a few feet from the device.

Whatever invisible ropes had tethered him to the puck before now had, it seemed, been severed during the time of his sojourn. He took a seat on the piano bench, swinging his legs under the instrument, and considered the keys. It seemed like he really might play something for us.

'What's beyond here?' somebody asked.

'Don't ask him that,' Pastor Wilky said, belligerent. 'There is no beyond.'

People chuckled.

'For *him*, I mean,' Pastor Wilky added quickly. 'There is no beyond for *him*.'

A note sounded. A piano note. We all looked to the reJesus. Where else? There was no other piano in the church, and the note had vibrated quietly, yes – but also clearly.

Now, you will find those among us who say they actually witnessed reJesus pressing a piano key, and you will find those who claim his hands never left his lap. Similarly you will find a contingent who insist the note was a B flat. Others, an A. But let it be known that there was – and is – complete agreement that a note did sound. That much we can state with certainty, that much we feel comfortable presenting to you as a fact. Even Bunny will tell you she heard the note. As for what you should make of that, well . . .

'I'm afraid you won't find much you like beyond here,' reJesus said.

We waited for him to say more, obviously.

'What's that mean?' Pastor Wilky asked. 'What do you mean by that?'

'If you can't love each other *here*, I highly doubt you'll figure out how to do it over there.'

'So there *is* an over there, then,' Buck Newlin said, a tad too triumphantly.

'Over there, here, same difference,' reJesus said. 'You have no idea where you are anyway.'

Once again, none of us seemed to have any clue what he was talking about.

'I'm not sure this is accurate,' Delia Cross said. 'Theologically, I mean. The real Jesus never said anything like this.'

reJesus sighed.

We looked at the puck at the base of the stairs. Was it possible God was reaching out to us through it? Bunny emerged from her pew and stepped forward. She was wearing sweats again and the gray roots in her hair were showing. She had, earlier that week, put her duplex on the market and there was a rumor going around that she'd quit her job too.

'Bunny,' reJesus said. 'You ready?'

She nodded, and reJesus processed down the aisle, a placid look on his face, and moved toward the exit.

'Where are you going?' somebody asked.

'Out,' he said.

He ghosted through the double doors at the rear of the church. Bunny followed after him in her flip-flops. A handful of us – nearly half – slid out of the pews and hurried down the aisle, chasing after them, curious to find out what he might do next. Outside the church we saw him across the road, walking through a field of freshly mowed green grass, the sunlight penetrating his robe as shafts of transparency. Bunny was only a few steps behind him. We hustled after them, the wet grass sticking to our shoes and pant hems.

At the edge of the field, where it met another road, he turned to us and announced that he was leaving us behind. He was going somewhere we couldn't follow because, absent faith, we'd find only darkness and confusion. We were visitors here, and one day we'd understand the truth of it. But until then death would toss us down into a vast black sea that would swallow and churn and drown us back to life again. *This* life. This dream. We'd wash up on the shore of this dream over and over again until we learned that we belonged elsewhere and to another. Over and over again, thrown back, we'd find ourselves in the warm, comfortable wombs of our mothers, where sticky clusters of cells would blossom and entrap us and make us think we were Eliza Wheelers and Bunny Mayhews and Buck

Newlins and Pastor Wilkys. We would never be able to cross that dark sea and find home unless we first –

He was gone! Fizzled away like a mist of rain over hot concrete.

'What was he going to say? *Unless we first* – do what?' someone asked.

'Do you think he . . . ?'

We looked up to the sky but saw only clouds and sun. No angels, no staircases. Beautiful – but ordinary.

And where was Bunny? She was nowhere to be seen, and for a moment it really did seem possible she'd disappeared with him, gone wherever he'd gone. Then somebody spotted her farther down the road, walking alone through the parking lot of a grocery store. We watched her until she reached the end of the lot and just kept on going.

'Maybe he ranged too far from the device,' someone suggested.

Curious, we returned to the church, hoping that perhaps he'd been lassoed back into place above the device and might continue his lesson there. Instead we found Pastor Wilky and a few others hunched over the baptismal font. We crowded in, each of us, to see for ourselves, the puck, drowned at the bottom of the shallow marble tub. The little green light at its top was no longer blinking. The damage was done. ■

The latest from *Granta*'s International Editions

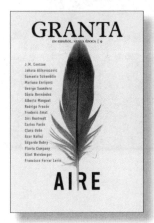

Courtesy of Bridgehampton Tennis and Surf Club / John-Paul Teutonico Photography

VOWS

David Means

I never caught exactly what was said about us and could only imagine the vicious forms the rumor took as it started at the church and jumped from house to house along the river, somehow making the two-mile leap over Tallman Mountain State Park as it headed to the town of Piermont where the Dickersons lived, and then from Jenny Dickerson's mouth up the river several blocks, skipping the Morrison house (she was rarely home), most likely to Sue Carson, and then from her mouth to Andrew Jensen, the rector at St Anne's, who, I still liked to imagine, spiced the rumor with some biblical flavor, somehow couching his comments in theological terms, mentioning the fall and temptation and the sins of adultery and so on and so on as he passed it to Gracie Gray, who tasted all the possible ramifications, twisted it even more to make me into a villainous antihero, unaware that both of us, Sharon and I, had betrayed each other, and then held the story in her mouth for several weeks, where it sat until I turned from the window at our annual holiday cocktail party to find her looking at me.

In a teal dress, tailored square to her shoulders, cut low in a rectangle, framing pale flesh and her pearls, which swayed as she moved gently to the music, Gracie winked at me and then turned away coyly, rotating at the waist and letting her legs – I swear I remember this! – swing around in an afterthought, as if she were resisting a magnetic pull. Then, in exactly the same way, she slowly turned back and reconnected with my gaze and, while the midnight cold from the window behind me brushed my neck, we seemed at that instant to share an exchange.

Her side of the exchange seemed to be saying: *in your public retaking of vows a few months ago, you and Sharon exposed a crack in the facade – the happy couple! Ha! The perfectly wonderful family! – and although that crack has been sealed in a ceremony with new vows, it remains a crack.*

While my part of the exchange went: *I understand that you think the seal might still be weak, Gracie, but it's not, not anymore.*

Then she squinted her eyes at me and gave me a look that seemed to say: *don't flatter yourself, jerk. You're a creep. I'm simply offering you a little holiday gesture of flirtatious cheer to warm your lonely, pathetic soul, and, anyway, after hearing the rumor, and then passing it on to Stacy Sutton, telling her how you betrayed Sharon, I'll be the first one to pry you two apart, to weaken the seal. On the other hand –* she widened her eyes and then winked – *perhaps sometime in the future on a night like this – crisp and clear outside, with an almost artificial-looking rime of frost in the corners of each windowpane – with all of this good fortune in the air, well, who knows? Is there anything more dangerous than a full-blown sense of good fortune?*

Looking back, I think that we might've had a similar exchange – if you want to call it that – at the church, after Sharon and I kissed, as I swept the sanctuary from pew to pew to make sure everyone got a chance to witness the frankness in my face, because after we sealed our new commitment with a kiss I got a sense in the late-day light trying to come through the stained glass overhead, in the big brass cross behind me, in the way it felt to stand on the altar, that Sharon and I were being held up to a judgment that hadn't existed before the ceremony.

Before the renewal ceremony began there had been a new sense of mission between us, an eagerness that had disappeared as soon as we started reciting our vows. When we turned to each other, with Reverend Woo between us, and began speaking, it was in the subdued, somewhat feverous voices of two people who had reconciled after one final, devastating argument that had lasted several months, beginning one day at the beach in Mystic, Connecticut, with the Thompsons, who were down near the water when I turned to Sharon and said, All this pain will pass. We really can work this out.

And she said, I no longer care what Dr Haywood says. The middle ground doesn't seem to be available for us.

And I said, quoting Dr Haywood again, Gunner must be kept front and center. It's our duty to him to do everything we can to build a new life out of the ruins.

Down the sand, Gunner yelled, What did you say about me? Hey, hey, you guys, what are you talking about?

Sharon's face was soft, lovely, tan. Her eyes were pooling a sadness that I found attractive. Near the water, Carol Thompson, who at that time didn't have the slightest idea what was going on, was lifting her son up by the hands, swaying him over the water and dipping his toes into the surf.

Her husband, Ron, was a few yards down the beach, holding himself at a remove, shielding his brow as he serenely scanned the water. For a few seconds there was a shift in the air, Sharon was gazing out at the water and we both felt a stasis, a place where we could rebuild our marriage, and then the feeling disappeared – and Gunner called again, waving his blue shovel – and she leaned in and whispered, Fuck you, and I whispered, No, fuck *you*, and then I lay on my side and watched out of the corner of my eye as Carol lifted her son up and down (she had strong shoulders and long, elegant arms, and I felt, watching her, with the sand against my legs, the soft seep of ardor coming again).

Ardor was a word I used a lot back then when I talked to myself. Ardor's taking over, I said. The air is loaded with ardor this afternoon, I said to Gunner as I watched him, day after day, in the backyard.

Ardor's radiating from those trees, I said in a mock-British accent, pointing at the pines along the edge of the yard. Then he scrunched his face and gave me a look that said: *You're strange and silly, Dad. Whatever you're saying, it's dubious.*

His look seemed judgmental in the purest sense, as if he knew somehow that his mother and father had betrayed each other, parted ways, heading off into distant blissful worlds.

O n the beach that day in Mystic I rolled over and kept my face down and admitted to myself, as I do now, that it had been in the end inevitable, considering the amount of ardor – or ardor-related gestures generated – that the lust, or whatever, would congeal, or perhaps the word is incarnate, into an act of adultery on my part and, at almost the same time, on Sharon's part.

Sharon had confessed to me about her lover, the Banker, and I had confessed to her about Marie, whom she called the Teacher, and in those confessions we had each allowed carefully curated details in – the Standard Hotel on Washington Street, a few drinks after a long session briefing a client, a clandestine meeting in Piermont on a lonely, sad day in the fall when she was out in Los Angeles, time zones away. A Lorca poem memorized in Spanish. Funds transferred into an account managed by the Banker. The rest was left up to our horrific imaginations. I imagined her eating lunch with him, down the stairs, in one of those older Upper East Side establishments, with ivory-white tablecloths and candles flickering in the middle of the day. Outside the windows, I imagined the legs and high heels and shoes of those walking past while they whispered sweet nothings to each other, and felt the beautiful, clandestine joy of holding a secret together in Manhattan. What she imagined I can only imagine, but I'm sure she built images of me with Marie, images of her face drawn from parent–teacher conferences: the two of us leaning back on a blanket somewhere deep in the state park, looking up at the sky, smiling in postcoital quiet, watching the clouds meander over the river. I imagined that she imagined – as I did – lips hovering, dappled with sweat, just before a kiss. The faint, citrusy smell of her neck. The sweet moments between touch – a finger hovering just over the flesh. Exquisite pain, of course, came from these imagined moments because they were pure, clear, drawn from the mind's own unique desires.

At the beach that day in Mystic, with my cheek against the sand, I felt a keen injustice in the clichéd nature of our situation, that thinking it was a cliché was also a cliché, or maybe bringing it up as a cliché is even more of a cliché, and even more of a cliché to bring up the fact that a cliché is a cliché.

What are clichés but the reduction of experience into manageable patterns, Dr Haywood told us a few weeks later, during a counseling session. You call it a cliché, but the brain can only process so much.

That day in her office – on the ground floor of an apartment building on 96th Street, not far from the park – Dr Haywood explained that the brain's attention can only be drawn precisely to one thing at a time, and only those things the brain deems worthy. You catch a flick of movement in the grass, near the water's edge, and then you draw your attention to it if you deem it worthy, or else you let it float away and think: *that's just a bird alighting, or flying off, and I'm going to keep my attention on that boat, the leader of a regatta, tacking around a buoy, catching the wind in the belly of a sail.* Cliché, she explained, is the brain's way of speeding up cognitive analysis.

I lifted myself up and brushed the sand from my arms and leaned towards Sharon and said, Well, Sharon, we need to go back to our original vows and start from scratch, and she said, Honestly, I'm sorry to say but in retrospect the original vows didn't cut it in the first place. The original vows were obviously batshit silly.

She kept talking until Gunner came up along the sand, walking with his side-to-side sway, looking suspicious. For several days he'd been listening carefully as we spoke in a weird manner, keeping everything – as far as we could – cryptic.

Betrayal doesn't go away, Sharon said.

I'd like to find a firm footing. Something we can stand on.

What are you talkin' about? Gunner said. What about my foot?

Mom and Daddy are talking adult-talk. Sometimes adults have to talk adult-talk, Sharon said.

Then he began to pressure and pry and make us both deeply uncomfortable but also – it seems to me now, sitting here alone with my drink, watching the water – even more eager to find a language that might, without exposing our plight, also prove magically useful. We had to blur the details and speak in code and we ended up speaking in a kind of neo-biblical lingo.

I'm not sure we can make it up this hill.

The hill is made of your frickin' ardor.

No, no, the hill is a big-shot banker in Manhattan. We both climbed hills. We're both equally guilty.

What hill can't be climbed? I want to climb the hill with you, Gunner said, and in-between our words there would appear a hint of solace, of the reconciliation that would arrive if we simply continued speaking in code for the rest of our lives with our son between us, asking suspicious questions, redirecting our pain into his pale blue eyes, his tiny ears.

Anthony's Nose, one of us said, referring to the beautiful mountain north of the Bear Mountain Bridge. We're talking about taking a climb up Anthony's Nose.

I wanna climb the nose, Gunner said. His eyes were wide and resolute and sparked – it seemed – with a keen knowingness, a sense of playful desperation.

That afternoon with the Thompsons on the beach in Mystic, we began an argument that continued into fall, taking any number of forms: me in support of the original vows; Sharon against; vows dead and dried up and scattered forever in the dusty winds of our infidelity. Vows broken to begin with, tried, simplistic and never powerful enough to determine our future; vows subsumed to the weight of dead traditions, symbolic claptrap uttered from youthful throats that had been eager, ready to say anything (any fucking thing, Sharon cried) in order to instill a sense of permanency in the world.

We fought and eventually – in that strange way that one argument can lead to another and then to something that resembles silence – we reached the endpoint, at which point action is the only recourse.

But before we got to that point we had to go through a fight that night, after our trip to the beach, with our skin still salty and taut and Gunner asleep in front of the television set. While I argued in support of our original vows, taken years ago on a crisp, clear fall afternoon in the city, Sharon made the case – her voice deepening, shifting into her attorney mode – that those vows were dead and gone, used up, depleted, scattered forever on the cold wind of our infidelity.

A week later, at the top of Anthony's Nose, keeping Gunner close at hand, standing there with her hands on her hips and her chin up as if speaking to the sky, she explained that she thought our commitment had been flawed anyway, silly and traditional. We were just kids. We didn't know what we were doing.

On Anthony's Nose we were rehashing previous fights, looking down at the river where it went north past West Point, buried in the haze.

Sharon pointed out, her voice getting soft and gentle, that we had never really discussed ('had a sit-down' was the phrase she used) the wording of those original vows and had instead entrusted their composition to Reverend Moody (Judson Church in Washington Square), the same man who had married her parents back in Cleveland. We had seen him as a kind of good-luck token, because his words had sealed the covenant – I remember she argued that that was a much better word – that had led to *her* conception and then her existence and, via her existence, to our meeting by pure chance that day in the Boston Common, sitting on the same bench and reading the same book (*Pale Fire* by Vladimir Nabokov).

We bickered and fought and then finally renewed our vows at the little Presbyterian church in Snedens Landing, New York, about twenty miles north of Manhattan, on the west side of the river, tucked amid expensive estates – Baryshnikov lived back there, along with Bill Murray.

The Reverend Woo presided, leaning forward in her vestments, quoting Merton on humility (my contribution) and Robert Frost on roads not taken (Sharon's contribution), while Gracie Gray, John and Sue Carson, Joanna and Bill and Jenny Dickerson, Bill and Liz Wall, Karen Drake and Janet Smith, Jillian and Ted Wilson-Rothchild, and Sharon's mother Anna Rose, who had flown over from Tralee, Ireland, looked on as I repeated Woo's words back to Sharon – *for eternity, ever after, we renew these vows in the great spiral of time itself, the dark matter of our particular, unique love, tucked in the folds of the universe, marking our small minutia of time here out of the random chaos, uniting our love to a semblance of form, tightening ourselves against the timescape of our lives* – until it was my turn to listen to Woo speak Sharon's part of the vows and I tried to stay focused as she recited her part back to me, something about *the renewal of the original impulse of our love, returning to the original pulse of desire that is on this day consecrated* (I'm pretty sure she spoke both those phrases: *the original impulse* and then *on this day consecrated*).

Her side mentioned Gunner – something along the lines of *between us, shared, our devout love of our son, Gunner, stands.*

She listened to Woo speak a few words and then to me as I repeated those words, and then I listened to Woo speak and then to Sharon again and then we kissed each other with honest eagerness and stood arm in arm while out in the pews, next to Sharon's mother, who was dressed in a lime-green blouse and a pleated herringbone skirt, looking weary and jet-lagged after her flight across the Atlantic, Gunner stared at me with blunt blue eyes that seemed to say: *you have betrayed me, father, insofar as you had a part in my creation.*

Please don't think I'm trying to say, as I sit here alone enjoying the warm summer evening, alone in the house, and once again, for perhaps the thousandth time, studying the Hudson River, that we didn't renew our commitment with the most devout sincerity, or that retaking our vows wasn't the right thing to do at the time, or that it wasn't a pleasure to leave Gunner with Sharon's mother and drive away from the front of the church, in the verdant spring air, trailing a ridiculous string of rattling cans all the way through Queens to the long-term parking at JFK. But the look my son gave me, or at least the look I imagined he gave me, seemed to reveal that even *he* was aware that the renewal ceremony revealed, or rather exposed, a rending to our friends, to the public, to the world at large.

P lease, will you stop about the look Gunner gave you, Sharon said that night in Dublin. You're being ridiculous. He has no idea. If anything, he's happy for us.

She was at the window of our room in the Gresham Hotel, her back turned to me, looking down at O'Connell Street. It was a lovely evening with a breeze blowing through the window, brushing her hair around her shoulders. (Oh God, Sharon had the most beautiful auburn hair with natural highlights! And, oh, and those eyes, mercurial, quicksilver eyes that shifted with mood and light! Even now I can recall the look she gave me earlier that day in Dublin as we stood on a bridge and looked down at the Liffey – solemn and dark water below, which seemed to hold centuries of stonework and old barges and history going back to the Vikings, coming back up into her eyes as she gave me one of her sidelong glances, flirtatious and judgmental at the same time, and then she gave me her wonderful smile.)

At the window with her hands on her hips she was swaying gently, shifting her weight from one foot to the other. Come to bed, I said. I won't ever say that word again. It doesn't need to be said. I promise.

What word?

Vows, I said.

Oh, honestly, I said I don't want to hear that word ever again.

I stayed silent as we lay together in bed. We had walked aimlessly to stay awake, to fight off the jet lag, drinking coffee, surprised at the clean modernity of the city, arm in arm as we stood at Trinity Gate, which was closed, and strolled down Grafton Street – like any other mall in America, we agreed – to St Stephen's Green, where we found a bench and sat for a while and held hands like proper newlyweds. Then, as we meandered back in the direction of the hotel, we lucked upon Oscar Wilde's house, or at least I insisted, before we crossed the street, that it was Wilde's house. In reality it was his father's house. The confusion sparked a short, brisk argument – the first of our renewed marriage! – as we waited for the light to change. Sharon's voice had tightened and became litigious, resolute and pristine in a way I admired and loved. The argument began on one side of the street and ended when we got close enough to read the round plaque that described an eye surgeon and folklore expert, Wilde's father.

You were right, I told Sharon, feeling incredibly happy.

Then we had made our way back down O'Connell Street, stopping here and there to look at the shops, laughing and teasing each other about Oscar Wilde, and we ended up at the bar in the touristy pub next to the hotel, sitting shoulder to shoulder, still weary from jet lag, leaning like regulars into our pints and sipping together in unison, sharing for the first time a mutual loneliness (a kind of blissful isolation, a sense that we were united in our new bonds) that would – I now see – last for years, until we held hands in the hospital room and prayed softly together while outside the sky over the river charged up with particles and produced, somewhere over New Jersey, a bright flash of lightning.

W as it a cliché to have a second honeymoon in Ireland? Sure. Is it a cliché to link that one drink together in the pub, after our first fight at Oscar Wilde's father's house, with our relationship after our renewal ceremony? Is it a cliché to make the leap from that moment – when we were first feeling the deep unity between us that would last for years and years – to that final night in the hospital along the upper western edge of Manhattan, when I held her hand and felt the faint bud of pulse in her wrist and then pulled her hand to my mouth and began to weep?

Yes, perhaps. But what Haywood said to us that day in therapy stuck. To push further, as I sit here today I am sure that in the hospital – with blue sawhorses in the street set up by the police, and a summer thunderstorm brewing over Jersey – with our hands cupped gently, we both felt the beauty of our commitment to time itself, to something vast and eternal and, above all, secretive. It was ours and ours alone. Whatever rumors and hearsay and conjecture floated around our story, whatever people made of it from gathered fragments, could only intensify what we had together.

On a family trip out west years after the ceremony, watching the road taper into the horizon outside of Bismarck, North Dakota, I began to wonder if we had completely nullified each other's vows by renewing them. I theorized that Sharon's vows had simply canceled mine out, creating a different kind of void. Gunner was sixteen at the time, lurking in the back seat with his headphones on, and the sight of his bobbing head, with a halo of hair puffing around his headphone band in the rearview mirror, had been disconcerting. Looking drunk back there, with his eyes loose and formless, lost in his music, he could've been anywhere.

Next to me, Sharon slept with her head back and her mouth open. That's what I recall from our Grand Canyon trip. Sharon sleeping and my son, with his adult bones eagerly hardening beneath his muscles and his muscles pushing against the fabric of his sleeves, in the back seat, lost in his beloved death metal. Even at the rim of the canyon, looking down, taking in the vast expanse, all he did was nod his head slightly to the music in his headphones and casually brush off the sublime vista.

On the way home, I think, this theory of a complete nullification of vows came to mind.

As I drove, I balled the thought up – the theory of complete nullification – and threw it out the window. That's a meditation technique I was using at the time: take a thought, write it down on some mental paper, hold it, turn it around in the mind, center on it and then ball it up and throw it away.

Somewhere along a road in North Dakota, I tossed that thought out the window.

Now, sitting here, I imagine it's still out there, curled in the scrub and dust, waiting to be discovered and unfolded.

O ne night, standing over my son as he slept, while the snow swirled around outside, it struck me that if we ever had another renewal ceremony, a kind of third-time-is-a-charm deal, we'd have to simply act as our own authority before God and avoid all the formal trappings. (Those are the fun parts, Sharon said, her voice light and happy, when we were planning the second ceremony. The trappings are the part you're required to forget the first time you get married. We were too young, and uptight, and we forgot them. The point of a renewal ceremony is to have a deeper awareness and enjoyment and focus so you actually experience the trappings, she said. I said, I don't like the trappings, but you might be right. You've got to have some kind of sacred space overhead, some sense that the vows are being taken in a holy environment. Even if you get married on the beach, there has to be a consecrated vibe in the air, and she said, Yeah, right, with an edge to her voice, not bitter but not sweet.)

S haron and I are still uncomfortable with each other, I told my friend Ted one afternoon, before the renewal ceremony. We were out on the back patio, smoking cigars, facing the river. As the sun came in and out of clouds, the trees blazed with color and faded and blazed.

We're like a couple of crooks locked in a cell with a warden who looms over us to make sure we get along for eternity. We're both in for the death penalty, I said.

You're in for death, and so am I. Each meal is a last supper, he said, and we laughed. He and his wife Jennifer were astonishingly good cooks, master chefs, and their dinner parties were legendary. They weren't foodies. Their respect for food went beyond trends or fads. They cooked simple, elegant meals and knew how to set up a perfect party. Brisk fall nights with a hint of woodsmoke and harvest in the air. The windows of their house above the road, tucked in a notch in the palisade, flickering candlelight. Silver on white linen. Always perfectly balanced company, a few light-hearted guests, a sullen guest (Hal Jacobson, whose wife had jumped from the bridge), a blend of intellect, jest and despair brought together, drawn around a sense that the next dish would top the last, bringing all attention to the mouth and tongue.

No matter what was being said, no matter how happy the talk, no matter what grievances were exposed, the next dish brought the conversation to a satisfying lull.

Before the dish arrived, we'd be complaining about the town's new sidewalk design, or someone would bring up the so-called nunnery that was, at that time, proposed for the empty meadow lot up near Hook Mountain. (I would keep quiet about the fact that I owned the small parcel that was necessary for an easement. It would come out soon enough. One way or another, if the proposal moved forward and went through the planning-board review process, the need for an easement would come to light and, with it, the fact that I owned the land. Then the fact that the New York diocese was negotiating with me to purchase it would come out, too.)

I'm only kidding about prison, I said to Ted, who looked at me, took a deep draw, and released a cloud of smoke.

Ted was a federal judge and played the role even when he was off the bench, relaxing with a cigar in hand. He was the type who prepared his cigar in an old style, popping a nub out of the end of the cigar with his thumbnail, rejecting my clippers and then my expensive butane lighter – the flame powerful and invisible until it hit the tobacco and bloomed like a blue orchid – in favor of kitchen matches. Even when he was relaxed, he seemed to have the straight-backed reserve of a man who was withholding judgment, sticking with procedure. He took another draw on his cigar, kept his lips lightly around the wrapper leaf and spoke with firm authority, You're not in prison. If you'd rode the blue bus and then went through the security check at Rikers Island, you'd understand what it means to be in prison. But I get your point, he said.

Well, you should, I said. I knew he had gone through some serious marital problems of his own. On the porch – this was late fall, a cold wind coming from the north, hunched in our coats with our collars up, enjoying the feeling of smoking outside, as if we were in the Klondike, two rugged explorers stopping for a smoke, he knew and I knew at that instant, sitting there, that the next thing out of his mouth – or mine – would be a comment about the quality of the cigars, and then one of us would say something about the quality of the Cubans, and then one of us would tell a smuggling story. His that day was about how he once hid cigars – purchased in Europe – in his wife's tampon box to get them through customs, and I told him about replacing the bands, turning Montecristos into Dunhills, something like that, and then we settled into a deep ritual that betrayed time itself, turning the moment into something utterly simple and meaningless.

Years later, at his funeral, up on the hill across from the hospital, with the river broken gray slates through the trees, I'd remember that moment on the back patio and how he drew the attention away from my failure and allowed us to go back to the ordained pattern of our friendship, which had started with our weekly tennis matches. You want to play with a judge? I know this judge, and he's pretty good, someone told me. He's federal so he pretty much sets his own hours and can play with you in the afternoon, someone said.

In the years after the renewal ceremony the judge came to know the full story of my marital problems with Sharon. His son was at West Point for a few years, and I remember that he talked often of him, saying things like – *my son is a plebe, and right now, as we play tennis, he is, most certainly, being tortured into adulthood.* His son would become a captain and die in his second tour in Iraq, killed by an IED, but of course we didn't know that at the time.

O n the night of the party, months after the ceremony, Ted's loss of his son in Iraq was five years away, still up in the vapors, and he had no idea that it was ahead of him, and I had no idea that someday I'd look back and see both of us as we'd be years later and filter our friendship through that particular moment. Dare I say that as I turned and had that exchange with Gracie, and the judge glanced at me, we both sensed that in the future we'd look back at that moment? Ted's face as he held the cocktail shaker in his hands, had the placid look of authority, a look I had seen after one of his fantastic tennis serves, standing with his legs apart and his racket at his side, gazing over the net with honest humility. The ball had zipped past. The air was brighter, cooler on his side of the net and duller on my side. All of his efforts – the toss-up, perfectly placed, his racket going back to touch the crook of his massive back, his swing down to meet the ball, were gone, lost, and the serve manifested itself in the tink of the ball against the chain-link behind me and then disappeared into silence as it sat alone in the corner, nestled in leaves. That was the look he had when he turned to see me at the window, at our annual party, years ago.

Then he came over to where I was standing by the window and asked if I was okay. He had his hand on his shoulder and was leaning forward and his face seemed to be saying: *Yes, I'm holding you in judgment, old friend. I'll give you my verdict in a few years.*

True love is, when seen from afar, a big fat cliché. It is a glance from the side while looking down at deep water. A fight on a beach. A sweaty brow covered with sand. Lips between kisses. Betrayal eased into grace.

(Let it go, Sharon said. You theorize too much about these things. How many times have I heard a witness claim that they told themselves to remember what they were seeing when the truth is they were too freaked out, or too scared, or even, in some cases, unaware that a crime was even transpiring.)

All I can say now is that I stuck to my word. I don't think we ever discussed our vows again. We settled into life. We shared everything together. After that night in the Gresham Hotel we went on finding places, situations, where we could simply sit side by side, shoulder to shoulder, lifting a glass in unison.

O ne evening, years later, we walked up Lexington Avenue after dinner with Gunner and his fiancée, through a hazy, dusky midsummer evening at the end of a preposterously hot day. The streets baking with heat. A giant sinkhole had opened in Queens. An unbearable glaze hung over everything. Cars dragging themselves through the glaze of Park Avenue. With sunset, a breeze had arrived, fragrant with the smell of hot pavement and something that smelled like cotton candy. We were walking hand in hand, sauntering, and after the dinner – the cute formality of Gunner across from the love of his life – we were relishing a sensation of success. We had raised a gentle soul, a man who tended to his lover's needs and had found someone who would tend to his, and that fact alone seemed sufficient.

Before meeting Gunner and Quinn at the restaurant, Sharon and I had gone to a museum, stood before a Picasso painting of a lobster fighting a cat, and then moved on to examine a Franz Kline, a few wonderful thick blue brushstokes splayed in cross-hatch, and then, downstairs in the cool lower level, a Van Gogh, a small, secret scene of a shadowy figure of a lonely woman, or a man, passing out of (or into) a pedestrian tunnel in the glow of dusk.

As we walked south that evening at a leisurely pace towards Grand Central, we were feeling a contentment that came from the fact that we had passed from the cool, secretive moment together before some of the finest works of civilization, out into the blazing heat, and then into a restaurant on Lexington, and then, two hours later, back out into a cooler dusk alone together.

Years after the fact, I can still feel the vivid sensation of seeing my own situation within the one that Van Gogh had selected for his painting, out of an infinite set of possibilities, and the feeling would linger with me for the rest of my life.

T hat night, somewhere in the sixties, or perhaps farther south in the fifties, we glanced to the right and saw what remained of the sunset, framed by the length of the street all the way to the Hudson, a slab of pure lavender light, gloriously perfect, combining with the cold, concrete edges.

That's as beautiful as anything Rothko painted, I said to Sharon.

(Oh dear, wonderful Sharon. Oh Sharon, love of my life. Oh beloved sharer of a million eternal moments. Oh secret lover of secret situations. Oh you who day by day shared a million intricate conversations.)

That vision has stayed with me. It illustrates how the window looks right now as I sit here with my drink, with the hazy deep blue light edged with the serene, pure black of the window frame, as I sit alone in a room, a year after that night in the hospital, thinking about my wife, about our life together while the river out beyond the window quivers and shakes with the last sunlight of the day. I have come to believe, in this time of mourning, that only in such moments, purely quiet, subsumed in the cusp of daily life, can one – in the terrible incivility of our times – begin to locate a semblance of complete, honest, pure grace.

In an average life lived by a relatively average soul, what else remains but singular moments of astonishingly framed light? ∎

SCHENECTADY

Adam O'Fallon Price

I have come to Schenectady to teach screenwriting to gifted high-schoolers. Written out, this sentence seems arbitrary, like a Mad Lib. *I have come to <u>Oaxaca</u> to teach <u>candlemaking</u> to <u>wealthy cannibals</u>,* say. Or, for that matter, I *haven't come to Schenectady to teach screenwriting to gifted high-schoolers* – that would make far more sense.

But it's true, David, it's all true. I'm here for seven weeks, at the talented and gifted program hosted by Newberry College, called, imaginatively, 'The Newberry College Talented and Gifted Program'. My second class is tomorrow and I'm writing from my hotel, a crummy dump outside of town called Suites of America. To be fair, it is near a waterfall; although, to be fair again, everything around here is near a waterfall.

My first class went poorly. I told them I was a screenwriter, and they asked me which movies I'd written. I mentioned *Save It for a Rainy Day* and they just blinked at me. Telling them I'd had quite a run in nineties independent cinema garnered the same response. Had they heard of independent cinema? Or cinema? The nineties? It was unclear. I finally told them that my old agency was the same as Robert Downey Jr's – Iron Man's, I made sure they knew – and on at least two occasions we'd briefly sat in the same reception area, and that he requested decaf red oolong tea and wore sunglasses inside, and this finally confirmed to them my bona fides.

Are they gifted? Time will tell. They are gifted with youth, at least, the greatest and most terrible gift of all. I feel so old these days, exponentially old, as though I age a decade each month, but I wouldn't want to be fifteen again, either. Their faces seethe with oil like the inside of lava lamps. They fidget and squirm like bored six-year-olds while the ugly truths of the adult world, like the ungovernable boners inside their cargo shorts, overtake them hourly without consent. They phrase everything in the form of questions, even their own names. Especially the girls – my God, the poor girls, who have to deal with the boys.

After class, one of the more talkative boys, Leonard – possessed of Jewish name and hair if not ancestry – approached and asked where he could find one of my movies. I asked if he had AMC, and if his parents let him stay up until four in the morning. He said yes, in fact, he did have AMC, and he lived with his grandmother, who let him get away with murder. I said, okay, then it might in theory be possible to see my movie *Drive By*. He said he'd keep an eye out, and I said that would be fine, and I looked forward to hearing what he thought. And he said he would take notes and let me know. He was refreshingly immune to irony, which gives a person hope in this cynical age, though he's probably just somewhere on the autism spectrum. Or maybe he was fucking with me, now that I think about it.

I walked the half-mile through town back to my hotel afterward. The class is at an expensive liberal arts college of regional repute. The campus is all rolling, manicured hills, and the second you step off of it, you're in *The Deer Hunter*. How did this happen, you wonder, staggering along with the other zombies through the post-industrial wreckage. But there was no industry here to begin with, how did they get to post so fast? I made my way past crumbling brick warehouses, past cleaned out auto yards, past an actual Moose Lodge with suspicious old men smoking Dorals in front. Despite the beautiful weather, I found myself palpably yearning for LA. Speaking of, how is it? You are in Glendale now, last I heard? Or was it Los Feliz? I'd so badly like to catch up soon, have that coffee we discussed, but I'm in Schenectady until August. August: it sounds like an eternity, and will be, I guess, but they are paying me well, hence my being here. They pay better than anything I could have gotten in LA, at least right now. Since getting tossed off *Murder Inc.* – did you hear about that? It was an ugly scene, and I'm here at least partly to lie low and get my head right. Or less wrong, although more on that later.

Or, okay, more on that now. Back to the hotel, I snorted the line I'd been waiting for all day, ever since the one I'd done in the morning. I'm on a strict regimen of two green pills a day – 100 milligrams – no more and no less. After lying for so long, to so many different people – first and foremost you, of course – I'm trying out what they call radical honesty. I relapsed again after our divorce was finalized, and I brought a large cache of oxy with me out here to cowtown. If my calculations are correct, it should be enough to get me through two months, provided I don't significantly up the dosage. It's a maintenance program, inasmuch as such a thing is possible, which of course it isn't. Radical honesty, David. Okay, maybe the program is that I'll either kick or die. That's probably the real program, probably the real reason I came here.

Please don't try to contact me, by the way. And don't try to find me. Names and places have been changed to protect the guilty. I may not really be in Schenectady. This may not really even be happening.

I tell the kids that the most important thing in screenwriting is to have a character that wants something. And I tell them this is harder than it sounds. The amateur tendency is to write characters that sit around on couches, talking to other characters on couches. Everyone loves writing dialogue because you can fill up the page so fast, the rising black like smoke signals in the middle of a whiteout blizzard. I love it too, I admit, but at a certain point, you have to get your protag (as I call it, horribly) off the couch and have them do something, something motivated by their desires. It sounds like the easiest thing in the world, but it's one of the hardest, like most things that sound like the easiest thing in the world: falling in love, staying in love, not ODing at your husband's parents' fiftieth anniversary party.

On the whiteboard, I diagram plot arcs loosely cribbed from *Save the Cat* and *Story*. I tell them each scene needs to have a positive and negative charge – that, in other words, something has to change. I tell them that this is true of scenes, and true of sequences as well, a progression of linked scenes. Sequences have to change, and so do acts, which sequences build, and so do screenplays, which are made of three to five acts, depending. I tell them that story is really about change, from the macro to micro level, and that, in this sense, a screenplay is like one of those images made from smaller constituent images of the same thing: a face, for example, but when you get closer you see the features are made of the same face, and closer still, that elements of the features – the shadow of a nostril, for example – is made of very small faces, and when you press your eyeballs up to those faces, you see a pixelated constellation of a thousand more faces. I tell them there's a word for this that has escaped me and that I'll give extra credit to anyone who tracks it down, which is ridiculous, as this is a talented and gifted summer camp, and there are no grades.

At that moment, I looked away from the board to find them all staring at me. I was very high just then, and I wondered if it was obvious. Probably not. As you well know David, being high on narcotics is so outrageous as to be somewhat unguessable to straight adults, let alone children. More likely they were wondering if I was insane. A girl raised her hand and said, 'I don't understand, Mrs Blakely.'

'Allison. Mrs Blakely's my chihuahua's name.' She stared at me. 'Don't worry about it,' I said. 'Just write something interesting' – really, the only good writing advice.

They addressed themselves to their computers for a thirty-minute free-write. I went to the bathroom, splashed water on my face, and got a Lipton iced tea from the vending machine. Did I feel bad about teaching class while high? Not at that moment, no – I was high. Besides, I was doing my job, more or less, and anyway, they wouldn't be able to get much more from me at 20 percent than me at a hundred. Frankly, the idea of teenagers writing screenplays, or any fiction, is ludicrous, a prestige class for the vicarious pleasure of helicopter parents. Nonetheless, I pushed back in and surveyed their projects: wizards and vampires mostly, though one kid had an idea for a buddy cop movie that probably could have sold for seven figures against mid-six. I made a mental note to rip it off, if I ever wrote another spec.

Did I tell you about the last thing I was working on, about the men who built the Brooklyn Bridge? Sandhogs they were called. They excavated the ground beneath the river and set the bridge's foundation inside these pressurized structures called caissons. Dangerous work: they were constantly injured, suffered from decompression sickness, and by the end of construction, twenty-one men had died. I had a meeting with one producer in Culver City who said he didn't see the drama, and another who questioned the sexiness of the project. I said, well, what if they worked naked? Then I found out there was another project, called *Sandhogs*, making the rounds with Edward Norton attached. That was the same week I called our showrunner a cunt, because he was one, and got fired. My agent said I had a reputation. A good one? I asked. No, he said, and your best bet would be to lie low for the rest of the decade. I told him I was broke, and he asked how I felt about teaching summer camp.

I am broke, David. It's remarkable to be broke after earning so much money. Where did it go? Well, we both know the answer to that. But in a more general sense, I suppose, it went to good times that weren't that good. I could have been building something – a family, a business – but instead, for the past twenty years, I've been building myself, an unlikely version of me. Tanned and ghostly pale, slender and puffed around the edges, hideously attractive, penniless but with the vague imprint of money – I stare at myself in the mirror, this creature I've painstakingly brought to life, Doctor Frankenstein and her monster, both in one body.

You asked me once, toward the end, after you'd discovered the withdrawals – the ones from our bank account, and the ones I was going through in that hotel room during one of my 'business trips' – why I did drugs. I told you that growing up in a loud and alcoholic household, I liked to enter the storage cubbyhole under our kitchen floor, where it was earthy and cool and dark and still, and pretend that everything outside had vanished, though I could hear the distant yelling, and that as an adult narcotics held a tremendous instinctive appeal, in the way it offered a quiet place to hide, though it was better than that cubby since you could take the still place with you wherever you went. But this was false. Oh, it may have been true years ago, but the need had long since become its own truth, the only truth that mattered.

Because the other truth, I guess, is that I don't see the point of all this, however you define *this*. From the outside, the drugs may seem to take away meaning, to confer a dead pointlessness to the proceedings; from the inside, however, it is just the opposite. They provide a titanium-grade purpose to my days, one that is knowable and achievable. Far from meaningless, dope is the greatest possible meaning, an absolutely defined value and good in a world of rumors and wraiths, fleeting desires and disappointments flickering incandescent against the void. It is nothing, but it is something. It is the somethingest nothing there is.

Leonard raised his hand in class today, and said, 'Self-similar.'
'Gesundheit,' I said.
'You asked the other day for the word for something made of things that look like itself. The word is "self-similar".' I had no idea what he was talking about. 'Great, Leonard. Thanks.'
'Do I get extra credit?'
'What?'
'You said whoever brought in the word would get extra credit.'
'Sure,' I said, 'you get a thousand points.' I went back to showing the intro to *Casablanca*, and rambling on about visual transitions.

After class, Leonard followed me down the hall and out into the shocking day. Summer was exploding in a mortar strike of bright, warm green, more shrapnel in my already still heart. If I could have felt anything at that moment, I might have been delirious with sadness or happiness, or both. I shivered in my thin jacket, in my invisible cocoon. Leonard said, 'You were being sarcastic back there.'

'No, I was being facetious.'

'Okay, I know I don't get extra credit, but I wanted to ask you a question?'

'What.' We were standing in the middle of a grassy slope, near a Japanese maple, and I had the horrible feeling he was about to kiss me.

'Will you come to dinner tonight? My grandmother would like to meet you.'

'Oh.'

'We only live ten minutes away.'

'I have plans.'

'I'll make guacamole.'

'Jesus. Sure.'

What else could I do? I went. Their house was unbelievable, David. One of those palatial, crumbling Victorians they have so many of in this part of the country, located off the long road winding into town, commissioned by some local magnate who must have promptly gone broke or insane. The thing had twenty rooms if it had two – did people used to have that many more children? I guess whole extended families used to live together. You can feel their ghosts in a place like this, all the high-collared dowager aunties and crib-dead kids still hanging out, making shadow puppets on the wall for entertainment.

It was just Leonard, clad in a dressy black turtleneck, and his young grandmother, Roxanne, only about ten years older than me. I didn't ask about the parents, but I got the sense they were still alive, somewhere on the periphery. It's hard to explain, but the house seemed like the wreckage of something, an aftermath. I got the sense something very bad had happened, and that what we had here were two survivors, shell-shock cases who had wandered, half-deaf and heads ringing, into the same cave. Or maybe they just didn't get many visitors.

Roxanne is a large, no-nonsense lady who has worked for the local electric company her entire adulthood. I liked her immediately. She has clearly made Leonard her project in life – saving for his education and sending him to things like the Newberry College Talented and Gifted Program – and she grilled me on my résumé.

'What a career,' she said, 'I'm very envious.'

'Yes, well,' I said. 'It's had some exciting moments, I guess.'

'You guess? You've had dinner with Jack Nicholson. Try operating a power company switchboard for forty years.'

'I know, I'm spoiled.'

'That's putting it mildly.'

'If only there had been someone to shoot me every minute of my life,' I said.

'What?' said Roxanne.

'Flannery O'Connor,' said Leonard proudly, and I was appropriately impressed, though less so by Leonard's guacamole, which, I have to tell you David, was sub-par – heavy on the lemon. Upstate guacamole, an oxymoron. Fortunately, I didn't have much of an appetite. I had forgone my evening installment in deference to the occasion, and I was not feeling very well. Thin trickles of sweat sluiced down the ice sheet of my back, as we all settled in the dark living room to watch the surprise Leonard had prepared. The TV clicked on to reveal *Drive By*, which Leonard had apparently, and incredibly, recorded off TV onto an old VHS tape. The vertical hold shuddered like my stomach throughout. After a brief Q and A about the script's genesis and the unholy litany of concessions I'd made to get it produced, I escaped back into the dark wilds of the front yard, in a near-sprint to get to my rental.

Attempting, with an extremely shaky hand, to fumble key into ignition, I saw Leonard's small form make its way through the shadows of the unmown grass. It felt not unlike that stock horror-movie scene, heroine dithering in the inexorable monster's path. Standing at the open window, he said, 'Are you okay?'

'Sorry,' I said. 'Not feeling well.'

'The guacamole?' he frowned.

'No, it was delicious.'

'Is there anything I can help with?' he said, and I wanted to cry. I cried. He stood there in adolescent alarm until I could speak. 'No, there's nothing. Thank you, it was great meeting your grandmother.'

Did I want children, David? I know I always told you I didn't, but did I, secretly? If not, why did I continue sobbing all the way back to the hotel, all the way through the dose, to the point of addressing the question to you, imaginary you? Are you glad we didn't? Are you going to do it with . . . Philippa? Can that really be her name? Are you going to have a little Silverlake family? Are you going to wear a Baby Bjorn at the co-op? Are you going to name the girl Hyacinth and the boy Elderflower? Is there any way to reclaim the time we've lost? Is there a place where our days aren't numbered? What is your worst fear? What is mine? And are you even reading this?

C hange is essential. I keep stressing that to them. Your characters must change, and you must change in the process. Because the best writing is not merely a finely crafted meshing of plot and character gears – though it is that, as well – it is an act of discovery in which the author finds out, by the time they type 'Fade Out', what their subject really is.

I am not so fucked up or deluded, David, as to think they really understand me now. My hope for this class – more accurately, the way I can justify dragging myself into the room every day and subjecting them to me – is that some spore of what I'm saying will catch in their heads, get buried in the shifting soil of their nascent neocortices, be watered daily by a wash of hormones, take root, and in time grow into a hardy little idea that cannot be pruned by convention or adulthood and its attendant demands: money, sex and ownership of stuff. The basic idea, I suppose, being the value of opening yourself to the world.

I can't remember a teacher saying anything that affected my thought process this way, but then again, I shouldn't be able to remember it, right? That's the point.

At any rate, yesterday I took them on a field trip (don't worry, I chartered a bus) to the nearest place of interest where they might not get murdered, an enormous shopping mall outside of Albany called, cryptically, Destiny USA. The assignment: pick one person who strikes your fancy and casually follow them, taking pen and paper notes on little notebooks I bought at the town drugstore along with a new set of syringes. Write down everything you notice about them: every mannerism, every smile, every phone call, every twitch or tic. I dispatched them like a police lieutenant putting cadets on the case. Then I went to the bathroom and got high.

The food court, at ten in the morning, was vaulted and luminous, a pleasure dome Kubla Khan himself would have admired, and sitting with my Sprite from Panda Express, I felt that here, nothing could really go wrong. Shoppers floated by, glazed with the many pleasures offered by mass consumerism, and I felt an unironic kinship with them, all of us seeking relief in our ways, bent beneath the weight of our lives. I drifted away beneath another kind of weight but was awakened by the scrape of chair against tile.

'Hey,' said Leonard.

'Aren't you supposed to be taking notes on someone?'

'I am,' he said, and I noticed the notepad in his hand, his eyes fixed on me.

I took a sip of my Sprite trying to clear my head. The soda was watery – how long, I wondered, had I been out? 'This isn't really in the spirit of the assignment.'

'Is sleeping in the food court in the spirit?'

'Touché. But please leave.'

He wandered off. After a minute or two, I walked out of the food court, to the edge of the second-floor mezzanine near the elevators. A young man in a green visor, reminiscent of the sort that old-style accountants wore, piloted a buzzing helicopter around. The mall was four stories, with an empty middle all the way up, and he directed the chopper into that airspace, out over the unsuspecting shoppers, and the first-floor fountain; then up and briefly level with the third floor, like a huge insect reconnoitering potential prey. No one seemed to notice, or care, not even the young man, who executed these moves with the bored, casual manner of a pro athlete warming up. He noticed me watching, and said, 'Wanna try?'

'I've never done it before. I'll crash.'

'No, you won't,' he said, 'I'll show you.' He put the controls in my hand, and, standing beside me, moved my thumb and forefinger on the correct levers. The helicopter dipped and juddered, but remained airborne. I could smell him, some kind of harsh adolescent musk and cigarette smoke. It was briefly, a tiny bit, sexy. 'See, easy. Dual stabilizers.'

'I won't be able to do it by myself.'

'You'll learn,' he said, pulling the controller back. 'Forty bucks. Thirty-five. Thirty.'

'Fine.'

I paid him and took the helicopter with me. I couldn't tell you, David, what exactly it was, but there had been a thrill watching it swoop and hover, a simultaneous death wish and denial of death. It had felt, for a very short moment, that I was somehow watching myself up there suspended in space. Again, I was very high. I met the kids at the prearranged spot, verified that none had been abducted, and slept the rest of the way back to campus.

I slept the rest of that day, and the next day, Saturday, as well. Today, I woke up and counted my doses. Six left, and two more weeks to go in the course. I showered and changed clothes, got high, and walked down the long dismal road behind the hotel, to a place called Overlook Falls, the edge of a state park that occupies the steep side of a ridge. It was a soggy day, somewhat cool for July, and only a few families wandered around the terminus of the falls, a small natural pool surrounded by rocks. I walked up the trail, a half-mile of steep and stumbly gravel, and came out panting on the fall's namesake overlook.

There was a fence around it, and I looked down, a seventy-or-so-foot drop into the white rocky mist. The fence's edge extended half-heartedly to the right edge of the cliff, seeming more like a suggestion than a command: *You probably shouldn't, you know, jump off this?* I easily moved around it and sidestepped back to the middle of the overlook on the thin strip of ground past the fence. I held the fence behind me and looked down – describing this shabby little melodrama is embarrassing, David, but I wanted to know what I would feel in this moment, where to fall would be as easy, easier, than to hold tight to the green fence and stay alive. Would it suddenly feel obvious?

It didn't. I moved carefully back around, aware that the only thing worse than jumping would be deciding not to jump and accidentally falling off. I shambled back down the ridgelet in a fog of narcotic shame, although what's new? So, I suppose on Wednesday, after my last dose, I kick.

Today is Sunday, the next one. The last week – well, maybe the less said the better. I told the program administrators that I needed a few days off, that there had been a death in the family. Or would be, I thought, lining up my Enfamil, my towels and cold compresses and ginger ales, my paltry analgesics and lozenges on the bathroom counter. Only six hours in, and I felt like road kill – not the recently dead kind, an animal's corpse, but the purplish blistered remains, hide and bone baking in the asphalt sun. I couldn't imagine it getting worse.

A mere sixty-six hours after that, it stopped getting worse. I'll spare you those three days, and spare myself the recollection in the process, though there isn't much that I remember. Pain is a kind of hypnotic, with amnesiac properties. What do you remember from your worst fever? The rim of your consciousness pokes out of the dark ground, sees its own shadow, and quickly descends again.

I kept some chicken noodle soup down today and went for a creaking walk around the grounds, threading my way between the wilting trees that ring the empty parking lot. It was hot and lovely outside, though I'm in the grip of the blackest depression I can remember. I have no endorphins now – they long since packed up and left, like elderly Jews heading to Boca Raton. Whatever pleasure is available to me exists in the form of relief from pain, but that's a relief that ebbs with disappointing speed. A car full of teenagers and teenage music zoomed by up on the road, and I wondered what they saw. A middle-aged woman in yoga pants holding herself by the shoulders, rocking gently back and forth in the shade of a sapling.

Leonard showed me his screenplay-in-progress. It is about an ill man, who keeps getting sicker and the doctors can't figure out why. He's at death's door (the title: *At Death's Door*), when they discover a small alien being that has burrowed into his abdomen. That's all Leonard had so far.

'What's next,' I said.

'That depends,' he said.

'On what,' I said.

'On if he decides to have it removed.'

'Why wouldn't he have it removed?'

'I don't know, maybe he's gotten used to it. Maybe he likes it,' he said, and looked at me meaningfully. We were working outside today, or 'working', the students spread out here and there with their laptops on the long, sloping lawn. A breeze shivered the grass down the hill, and I thought how strange it is that you can see the movement of this great, invisible thing, although maybe that's not strange at all, and I just haven't been paying attention to things like that. I am suddenly, horribly, alive, although that might be not having slept in almost a week. Colors assault me like loud sounds. I feel everything.

'Is this supposed to be about me?'

He shrugged. 'I don't know. Partly, I guess.'

'What do you think you know about me?'

'Just what I've observed. And stuff online.'

'What stuff online?'

'The *Hollywood Reporter*.'

'Jesus.' I looked at him, and he looked right back at me with a burning pride, not afraid at all. It's odd how a thirteen-year-old boy can be so much a child, yet already have assumed the mantle of adulthood, the man they'll become clearly visible – the child being the father of the man, and blah blah. Don't worry, David, I'm not going to show up in the news impregnated by a talented and gifted student. But Leonard is going to be a great guy, a fucking mensch, that much is clear.

He said, 'Anyway, it's easy for me to tell. Mom had problems too. Has problems.'

'Everyone has problems,' I said.

'Not like this,' he said.

'Well, no.' The grass riffled again. 'I'm trying. Don't tell anyone.'

'I won't.'

'Have the doctors take the alien out.'

'Okay.'

'Hey,' I said. 'After the session's over, you want to bring Roxanne over to my hotel suite for dinner? I'll cook.'

'Sure,' he said. 'That would be wonderful.'

In my hotel kitchen's tiny joke oven, I made the only meal I make very well, roast chicken and root vegetables. Roxanne and Leonard showed up twenty minutes early and watched TV while I cooked. We all had wine with dinner, including Leonard – the semester had ended on Friday, and it felt valedictory. We toasted to a job well done, to Leonard, to art, to summer in Schenectady.

I shouldn't have had the wine – I shouldn't ever have anything anymore. It made me want to get high. As I sat there, listening to them talk, the old urge bloomed like a black flower at the base of my spine, the thorny nettles scratching my innards and bringing on that unitchable itch. Or was it unitchable? I remembered that maybe, just maybe, there was an extra pill or two in the lining of my suitcase, that maybe, just maybe, I'd squirreled them away there for just such an occasion, and intentionally forgotten about it, such is the awesome strength and rigor of the addicted mind.

In the darkened bedroom, I groped around in the suitcase, thinking surely not. But the baggie came out like a wish fulfilled. In the bathroom, I crushed and cut the pills into powder, and it's hard to resist, in this retelling, the urge to cast the drug as metaphor, because opiates are all metaphor: life, death, sex, need, fulfillment, denial, dreams – a great big clipper ship going from this coast to that. I stood there over the sink for quite some time.

Roxanne begged off soon after I re-emerged, but I promised to get Leonard home safely. We'd planned on watching a movie – not one of mine, but *Dog Day Afternoon*, which he'd never seen. But when she left, I turned off the TV, and I said, 'You up for a field trip?'

'Sure,' he said.

I handed him a bag to carry, and he looked at it funny but didn't say anything, sensing he probably shouldn't ask any questions. We walked down through the lobby, and out into the night. Night here is real night, David, not LA's artificial night, day's insomniac half-sister. I mean stars blinking out their code, I mean owls making real owl sounds. We walked down the road behind the hotel, feeling like thieves, or at least I did. I have no idea what he felt – probably apprehension, as well he should have.

We ducked under the chained-off gate, into the park, and his worry must have mounted as he followed me up the trail in total darkness, slipping up, up the side of the ridge. But still he said nothing, and I realized, halfway there, the most wonderful and improbable thing: he trusted me. Against all odds, reason, or evidence to that point, he trusted me. We came to the lookout and stopped. Thousands of tons of water rushed below, unseen. I removed the helicopter from the box, and I handed him the remote control. Even in the dark, I could make out the curious look on his face, the question mark nearly visible over his curly head.

'You're going to fly it,' I said.

'Where?'

'Up, and out over the falls, and back.'

'I've never done it before,' he said, 'I'll crash.'

'No, you won't,' I said. 'It's easy, let me show you.'

'Okay.'

I put the controller in his hands, put my thumb over his, and together we piloted it slowly up. It hovered above the overlook, tiny searchlight touching the leaves behind us. We rotated it, and moved it gently out into the open air, the wet crashing air above the falls. Ten, twenty, thirty feet away. It fell, then rose on an updraft, higher and higher, spun and yawed and steadied again. Leonard looked up, rapt – God, I loved this kid. I sensed our held mutual breath as we gently rotated the chopper back toward us.

It seemed so important to bring it down safely, where we stood; it seemed life was paused as we inched the toy forward. But I understood, David, that life was already happening right there. Between survival and death, between despair and absurd joy – I saw that rather than needing resolution, this uncertainty was the entire point. Life was already happening right where we hovered, out there suspended over the void. ■

CONTRIBUTORS

Nuar Alsadir is a poet, essayist and psychoanalyst. She is the author of the poetry collections *Fourth Person Singular*, a finalist for the 2017 National Book Critics Circle Award for Poetry and shortlisted for the 2017 Forward Prize for Best Collection; and *More Shadow Than Bird*. She is a fellow at the New York Institute for the Humanities and works as a psychotherapist and psychoanalyst in private practice in New York.

Julia Armfield is a fiction writer from London, author of the story collection *salt slow*. Her work has been published in *Lighthouse, analog magazine, Neon* and *The Best British Short Stories 2019*. She was commended in the 2017 *Moth* Short Story Prize, longlisted for the 2018 Deborah Rogers Foundation Writers Award and was the winner of the 2018 *White Review* Short Story Prize.

Jem Calder was born in Cambridge, and now lives and works in London. His story 'Distraction from Sadness is Not the Same Thing as Happiness' was published in the *Stinging Fly*'s 2018–2019 Winter issue.

Te-Ping Chen is a writer based in Philadelphia. Her first book of short stories, *Land of Big Numbers*, will be published in 2021 by Houghton Mifflin Harcourt in the US and by Scribner in the UK.

Philip Gabriel is professor of Japanese literature in the Department of East Asian Studies at the University of Arizona. He has translated several works by Haruki Murakami, including the novels *Kafka on the Shore, 1Q84* (with Jay Rubin), *Colorless Tsukuru Tazaki and His Years of Pilgrimage*, and most recently *Killing Commendatore* (with Ted Goossen). He was the recipient of the 2001 Japan–US Friendship Commission Prize for the Translation of Japanese Literature for Senji Kuroi's *Life in the Cul-De-Sac*, and the 2006 PEN/Book-of-the-Month Club Translation Prize for *Kafka on the Shore*.

Matthieu Gafsou lives and works in Lausanne, Switzerland. After completing a master of arts in philosophy, literature and cinema at the University of Lausanne, he studied photography at the School of Applied Arts in Vevey. He has participated in numerous group and solo exhibitions, and has published five books.

Daisy Hildyard's first novel, *Hunters in the Snow*, won a Somerset Maugham Award in 2014 and a 5 Under 35 honorarium from the National Book Foundation. Her latest book, *The Second Body*, is an essay on the Anthropocene. She lives in North Yorkshire.

Ben Lerner was born in Topeka, Kansas. He has received fellowships from the Fulbright, Guggenheim and MacArthur Foundations, among other honours. He is the author of three books of poetry (*The Lichtenberg Figures*, *Angle of Yaw* and *Mean Free Path*, collected as *No Art*), the monograph *The Hatred of Poetry* and two novels (*Leaving the Atocha Station* and *10:04*). 'The Spread' is an excerpt from his third novel, *The Topeka School*, forthcoming from Farrar, Straus and Giroux in the US and Granta Books in the UK.

Sara Majka is the author of the story collection *Cities I've Never Lived In.* She was a fiction fellow at the Fine Arts Work Center in Provincetown and now teaches at the Rhode Island School of Design.

Magogodi oaMphela Makhene was born in Soweto, South Africa. She is a 2018 MacDowell Colony Fellow and won the Elie Wiesel Foundation Prize in Ethics Essay Contest in 2007. In 2017, she was shortlisted for the Caine Prize for African Writing. Her work has appeared in *Ploughshares*, the *Harvard Review* and *Guernica*. 'Innards' is the title story in a forthcoming collection.

David Means is the author of five story collections and the novel *Hystopia*, longlisted for the 2016 Man Booker Prize. His second collection, *Assorted Fire Events*, was awarded the 2000 *Los Angeles Times* Book Prize and was a finalist for the 2000 National Book Critics Circle Award. His fiction has appeared in many publications, including the *New Yorker*, *Harper's*, *Esquire* and *The Best American Short Stories.* He teaches at Vassar College.

Haruki Murakami was born in Kyoto in 1949 and now lives near Tokyo. His work has been translated into more than fifty languages, and he has been the recipient of a host of international awards and honours including the Franz Kafka Prize and the Jerusalem Prize. He has also received honorary doctorates from the University of Liège and Princeton University.

Adam O'Fallon Price is the author of the novels *The Grand Tour* and *The Hotel Neversink*. His short fiction has appeared in *Harper's*, the *Paris Review*, *VICE* and elsewhere. He lives in Carrboro, North Carolina.

Thomas Pierce is the author of *The Afterlives* and *Hall of Small Mammals*. A recipient of the National Book Foundation's 5 Under 35 award, his stories have appeared in the *New Yorker*, the *Atlantic*, *Zoetrope* and elsewhere.

Amor Towles is the author of the *New York Times* bestsellers *Rules of Civility* and *A Gentleman in Moscow*. Having worked as an investment professional for over twenty years, he now devotes himself to writing full-time in Manhattan, where he lives with his wife and two children.